MAY / 21 / 2007

A COMPACT HISTORY OF MEXICO

Daniel Cosío Villegas
Ignacio Bernal
Alejandra Moreno Toscano
Luis González
Eduardo Blanquel
Lorenzo Meyer

A Compact History
of Mexico

Foreword by Robert A. Potash
Translated by Marjory Mattingly Urquidi

El Colegio de México

Third reprinted in English, 2004
Second reprinted in English: 2002
First reprinted in English: 2000
Third Edition in English: 1995
Second Edition in English: June, 1985
First Edition in English: October, 1974
First Edition in Spanish: August, 1973

Ilustration: Mayan Priest from the Island
of Jaina, *ca.* 600 to 800 A.D., terra-cotta
Fotograph: Jorge Contreras Chacel

CONTENTS

7

FOREWORD

MEXICO IS ONE REGION of the world that has always fascinated strangers. Some, like the Asiatic nomads of 35 000 years ago and their successors, or the Spanish conquerors of the sixteenth century and their successors, came to settle and make their distinctive contributions to the evolution of Mexican culture and society. For others, especially today, Mexico is a country whose richness of experience, whether in terms of the conflicts of the past, the challenges of the present, or the promise of the future, stirs the imagination. Artists and scholars, students, and public-policy makers, and just ordinary citizens find themselves intrigued by and attracted to this country.

For the English-language reader who either in anticipation of a trip to Mexico or simply as an intellectual experience searches for a brief but authoritative treatment of the entire sweep of Mexican history, there is a poverty of choice. To be sure, travel books abound, but these serve other purposes and are not to be confused with the works of historians. Serious scholars writing for an English-language public have indeed produced numerous volumes on Mexican history but these have tended to focus on particular aspects or periods. Over the years a few general treatments have appeared, some of them highly subjective, others textbook-like in character, all of them useful in their way.

What is unique about the present volume is not that it attempts to provide a panoramic view of Mexico from prehistoric times to the present, nor that it accomplishes this task in so brief a compass, but that this *Compact History of Mexico* is the work of Mexican historians. Published originally under the title

Historia Mínima de México, its appearance now in translation enables English-language readers to see how a sextet of Mexican scholars, one an archaeologist and five historians, view the unfolding of their country's past. For the non-Mexican reader the availability of this fresh perspective is of value over and above the intrinsic merits of the book.

In its Spanish version and in its present translation, the audience for which this volume is designed is the broad general public. Indeed, the chapters which comprise its contents were originally intended for a television series. Accordingly, each of these chapters constitutes a brief synthesis of the period to which it is devoted; omissions were inevitable and much detail ruthlessly eliminated in favor of giving emphasis to trends and themes. The result nevertheless is a coherent view of the overall process of change in Mexico.

A few words about the authors, beginning with Daniel Cosío Villegas (1898-1976), one of Mexico's most distinguished men of letters. The diversity of his interests and the range of his achievements are too extensive to list, but it might be observed that the elegant ease with which he synthesizes Mexico's modern period (Chapter IV) is not unrelated to the fact that for over twenty years he was involved in the publication of the multi-volume *Historia Moderna de México,* itself a landmark in the writing of Mexican history. Alejandra Moreno Toscano, Lorenzo Meyer and Luis González of El Colegio de México and Eduardo Blanquel of the National University of Mexico represent a younger generation of historians whose scholarly works have won them acclaim at home and abroad. From the field of archaeology is Ignacio Bernal, author of the chapter on the prehispanic period. Dr. Bernal is widely known as a scholar and an administrator. Prior to becoming Director of the National Institute of Anthropology and History, he was for years Director of Mexico's world-famous National Museum of Anthropology in Chapultepec Park, where may be seen, in the original or in reproduction, many of the works of art and architecture discussed in his chapter.

The final pages of *A Compact History of Mexico* deal not with the past but with the present. They direct attention to some of the major problems confronting Mexico today and suggest a reorientation of existing tendencies. Although addressed primarily to the Mexican public, anyone interested in the future of that country would do well to ponder these suggestions.

ROBERT A. POTASH
University of Massachusetts

I. THE PRE-COLUMBIAN ERA

Ignacio Bernal

1

THE ORIGINS

THERE HAVE BEEN SEVERAL discoveries of America, some by chance and some by error. Of all these discoveries, only two have had far-reaching consequences. The first, which is the one we shall deal with, populated the continent. The last and most famous was accomplished by Columbus with his fleet of three sailing vessels at the end of the fifteenth century.

Columbus believed that he had arrived at eastern Asia or, more precisely, its offshore islands; and not until the early part of the sixteenth century did the Spaniards realize that the continent in question was one whose existence they had not previously suspected. The immediate problem—today it would be considered a scientific one but at that time it was mainly religious—was to establish the origin of the inhabitants of these new lands soon to be called "America." According to Christian doctrine, all the peoples of the world were descended from the first man and woman created by God; therefore, from which of the known human groups was American man descended? Although numerous theories were advanced, the passing of time and increased knowledge have disproved all but those of a few scholars like Father José de Acosta.

Using very different methods, scientific studies attribute another origin to the American man. The vast majority of these studies conclude that he gradually occupied America in a series of small migratory waves through the northwest tip of the continent by crossing what is now the Bering Strait. Today the strait separating Asia from America is fifty miles wide with two islands located about midway. Although not impossible, the crossing would have been extremely difficult for primitive man. However, it should be recalled that during countless millennia and until some ten thousand years ago this planet underwent variations in temperature due to complex causes that produced periods of great heat and great cold. During the latter period, called the "Ice Age," polar ice caps extended to lower latitudes. As the water froze oceans dropped as much as three hundred feet below their present levels. During this period, the Bering Strait, which is only one hundred and fifty feet deep, could be crossed on foot. Even the bitter cold and permanent ice were no deterrent to the Mongoloids of northeastern Asia, who had adapted to a way of life and developed a modest culture that enabled them to survive such a harsh climate.

Recent data suggest that Asiatic men began to enter America about 35,000 years ago. They would hardly have shouted with joy that they had discovered a new continent. They themselves could not know that their pursuit of some animal had taken them into what is today a body of water but what was then solid land stretching some fifteen hundred miles. Nevertheless, the same ice that formed a bridge to Alaska constituted a barrier to the rest of America. Only by taking advantage of warmer periods and striking out in different directions could these early groups go southward reaching regions that obliged them to change their culture and way of life in a long process about which we still know little.

As slow as these movements were, Patagonia was already populated 9,000 years ago and other parts of the continent even earlier. Primitive man was acquainted with fire and used stone tools to make clothing from animal skins and to carve objects of wood and bone. He probably also wove baskets and nets to snare fish and small animals. There is some doubt as to whether he hunted with bow and arrow or whether his only weapon was the sling.

With this rudimentary cultural equipment, man began to develop different ways of obtaining food according to local conditions, a task that was not only basic but time-consuming. Many of these groups lived essentially on wild plants and fruits and small animals; others became fishermen living from the sea; while others became hunters and trappers of large game. These specializations were not necessarily fixed and each group wrested whatever it could from its surroundings according to the season.

In these conditions, man was nomadic although he did not cover great distances. Families, joined together for some such purpose as a big game hunt, formed small bands with a permanent base. As they were all related, they had to marry members of neighboring bands. It is hard to imagine the life or even the mentality of such primitive men. Furthermore, they left few objects and still fewer have been found, many of these by chance. Therefore, our reconstruction of this remote past must be sketchy.

In Mexico, the excavations of Tlapacoya near Mexico City show that man existed here some 21,000 years ago. All we know about this man is that he hunted, had tools made of obsidian, and used fire. Discovery of the Tepexpan man, who lived 7000 years B.C., was very important because not only his tools but parts of his skeleton were found. The findings in Santa Isabel Iztapan, in Aztahuacan, and in Chicoloapan in the Valley of Mexico date from various periods, all very distant. A few human remains and stone implements tell us little about these people except that man existed in the Mexican highland at that time.

Recent excavations in the Tehuacan Valley furnish us with a historical sequence dating from around 7000 B.C., when man was both hunter and forager, as well as trapper of small animals. It would appear that he gathered about half his food from wild plants. He lived in small groups, moving about frequently with the seasons. His stone tools, although primitive, were adapted to different purposes. Like the first men to come to America, he carved wood and wove ropes, nets, and baskets, and perhaps even a crude cloth, although he certainly used skins for clothing.

About 5000 B.C. the population in the Tehuacan Valley increased. Additional wild plants, changing with the seasons, were added to the basic diet. More important, there is evidence of an attempt at cultivation, although still far from agriculture. There was a greater variety of implements and further utilization of natural products as well as the start of ritualistic burials and possibly human sacrifice.

By 3500 B.C. man had begun to farm, planting and harvesting corn, beans, squash, chili pepper and perhaps some fruit trees; but his diet still consisted chiefly of animals and wild plants. As the population continued to increase, many more tools were fashioned.

Better techniques were used for weaving nets and baskets and for making a wide variety of stone objects. The *metate* (a slightly concave grinding slab used with a long pestle), which is still in use, appeared for the first time and gradually replaced the stone for grinding. Although partly nomadic, each group probably lived a good part of the year in a permanent location, joining together several bands who only dispersed when the available food supply was exhausted. Although man tended to live in a fixed place, these places could not be called villages.

A thousand years later this way of life underwent an important change when groups of people dwelt all year round in semisubterranean houses constructed in river terraces. This was made possible by man's increased agricultural production, which included new food crops and came to represent a fifth of his diet.

Although such a low fraction would seem to indicate that little was sown—which was partly true—it was also due to low productivity. We think of corn, by far the most important plant in the agricultural history of Mexico, as the large ear with tightly packed grains that is grown today. But in those days, ears of corn were only a very few inches long with tiny scattered grains. Many ears would have been needed to make a tortilla. Over a long period of time this plant was developed into the Mexican's basic food crop. It eventually acquired a religious significance and 3500 years later Toltec legends would relate that Quetzalcoatl, the great cultural hero and source of all material and spiritual progress, also gave man corn, having stolen it from the god of the underworld.

A few centuries later the first pottery appeared, chiefly in the form of *tecomates*, *cajetes*, and *ollas* (differently shaped bowls), as well as small moulded figures that were later to become abundant. Nevertheless, quantities of stone vessels, sometimes very carefully worked, were still produced.

In the following phase of Tehuacan Valley, from 1500 to 900 B.C., an agricultural economy was fully consolidated. Man became a year-round farmer who lived in clusters of huts that sometimes reached the size of a hamlet. His house was of wattle daubed with mud and covered with a palm-thatched roof. In addition to the domesticated plants already mentioned, he grew *chía* (a kind of salvia), avocado, sapodilla, as well as cotton, from which he made cloth much finer than any he had formerly woven from the fibers of the maguey (century plant).

Once his sedentary life was established, with agriculture taking precedence over earlier activities, man expanded his artifacts to include a large number of carved and polished stone objects. He began to produce pottery, which was well made but limited to the forms mentioned above, and abundant figures not only of the small, crude, solid type but also ones that were much larger and hollow. These latter showed the influence of the Olmec culture which was developing on the coast of Veracruz and which was to raise all of Mesoamerica to a level of civilization far beyond anything attained by the inhabitants of Tehuacan Valley, whose history we have just outlined.

Although our information derives principally from that area, there is evidence that a similar, but not identical, process was taking place elsewhere and that the southern half of Mexico and the north of Central America were surpassing their neighbors in establishing a sedentary, agricultural society with a tribal organization. On the other hand, the appearance of clay figurines and ritualistic burials does not necessarily indicate a religion, which was to come later, but the existence of a magic that would serve partly as a base for and would be deeply involved in the culture of the area we call Mesoamerica or Middle America. It was in this area that civilization was launched, shortly before 1000 B.C.

2

THE OLMEC WORLD

IN THE RURAL, still primitive, world described in the preceding chapter, a series of basic changes took place which would produce the urban world later to dominate Mesoamerica. These changes occurred in various zones: Oaxaca, Chiapas, the Pacific coast of Guatemala, and especially the coastal region of the Gulf of Mexico which today forms the southern part of Veracruz and the adjacent Tabasco.

Except for the mountainous mass of the Tuxtlas, which averages 1,500 feet in altitude, the region is flat. It was formed by the silt deposited by large rivers descending from the mountains, and during thousands of years it expanded into the Gulf itself. For this reason, it is an alluvial plain without stone. Covering about 7,000 square miles and defined as much by culture as by geography, it is known as the Olmec region and the people who lived there during the thousand years before Christ are called Olmecs. Actually this is a misnomer because historically the designation corresponds to more recent groups and is a Nahuatl word, a language not spoken at that time. Olmec means "The Dweller in the Land of Rubber." Even today this region, unlike most of Mexico, receives heavy rainfall and is crossed by great rivers that cause frequent floods. At certain times of the year, numerous lagoons and swamps lend it a semiaquatic appearance. These environmental factors must have influenced the development of the Olmec people in various ways.

It is estimated that 350,000 people lived in the region. This number may now seem very small but it was enormous in the light of their modest agriculture, which was based on slash-and-burn cultivation. They did not use irrigation. When the land became unproductive after a few years, they would open up new parts of the forest. On the other hand, they could obtain good crops along the river banks and they also hunted, fished, and foraged. Apparently, population pressures drove the Olmecs to find other sources of livelihood, which we shall discuss later. These changes, in turn, obliged them to create a new social and political organization.

So far not a single human skeleton from this period has been found and our idea of the physical appearance of the Olmecs must therefore be based on their monolithic sculptures or figurines. We also have the present inhabitants of the region who, however much they may have changed, sufficiently resemble features shown in their ancient art to confirm the theory that the stone sculptures and figures were reasonably faithful representations of the people who lived there.

They were a short, stocky race, tending to be stout, with a rounded and chubby-cheeked face, and with slanted, puffy eyes clearly indicating their Mongoloid descent. Their nose was short and broad, their mouth thick-lipped and with the corners turned downward, and their jaw heavy. In sculptures their neck is very short or non-existent. These people achieved the remarkable progress that created Mesoamerica and its civilization.

The most important sites that have been explored are La Venta, San Lorenzo, and Tres Zapotes. Although very different from each other, common characteristics and similar objects furnish ample evidence that they belonged to the flowering of the Olmec world between 1200 and 500 B.C. In contrast with the scattering of humble houses found in the hamlets of Tehuacan Valley, their buildings for ceremonial use were erected according to a plan.

La Venta is the best example. The central line of the city—if we can call it that—runs from north to south, along which axis its monuments were located in a fairly symmetrical fashion. It is interesting to note that the great cities of the Mexican highland would follow this plan, rough as it was. Teotihuacan itself also would start with a north-south axis, apparently derived from the Olmec pattern. On the other hand, Olmec architecture was unpretentious because, for lack of stone, its buildings were made of clay, which was used in different colors to build pyramids of rather undefined forms. In La Venta huge natural columns of basalt were brought from the Tuxtla mountains and used to surround a central courtyard and to construct a monumental tomb suggesting a house made of logs. This type of architecture, with its limited possibilities, could not be successful and it was not copied in places where there was stone available for construction.

We know nothing about the houses of the common people or even of their chieftains. Probably they were made of wood or of mud-daubed wattle with palm-thatched roofs. The Olmec must have led a modest life, very different from that of Teotihuacan a thousand years later. Even so, for the first time man rose from a rural culture to the beginning of an urban life. This created a series of new and daunting problems that had to be solved.

Olmec sculpture rapidly reached a technical and artistic perfection never surpassed in Mesoamerica and perhaps only equalled by the Maya and Mexica. It is curious that the inhabitants of a region lacking stone should have been immortalized precisely for the great stone monoliths that they sculptured in profusion. Enormous blocks had to be brought in so that the Olmec artists could carve colossal heads, altars, stelae, and numerous other pieces, many of which have fortunately survived.

Best known and most spectacular, perhaps, are the enormous heads, of which thirteen have been discovered—the tallest being ten feet high. They are not incomplete statues but were conceived and executed as heads, just as an Aztec artist two thousand years later would sculpture the head of the Moon goddess. It has been said that they were portraits of chieftains or warriors, or monuments to the dead, or likenesses of gods. In fact, we are not sure of their real significance.

Almost as impressive as the heads are the monolithic altars, of which we have almost nine. They are rectangular and often with figures or scenes carved along their sides. A favorite theme is that of a personage who appears to emerge from a niche or a cave carrying a child in his hands. Other, very different, altars are decorated in front with atlantes in high relief. These are the most ancient examples of human figures supporting altars or roofs and would often be repeated later. But the Olmec atlantes are not sculptures in the round as the later ones at Chichén Itzá and Tula would be.

The stelae, no two alike, are, as their name would indicate, huge relatively straight slabs with motifs carved in low relief. The Tres Zapotes stelae include figures that may depict war scenes; but some of the La Venta stelae are the most beautiful, although in very poor condition. In Stela 2 a majestic figure wearing a lofty head-dress could be the forerunner of the priests and rulers of the Maya stelae. In Stela 3 there are two central figures of which one is particularly interesting because his features appear to be "Semitic" and therefore very different from those found in Olmec art. It has been suggested that this could be the likeness of a visiting foreign dignitary. They are surrounded by smaller figures full of movement and in every kind of position. Perhaps they represent the *chaneques*, those mischievous spirits who still frequently turn up in local folklore.

Although of a later period, the most important piece of this group is Stela C of Tres Zapotes. Unfortunately, its fragments are in two places, neither of which will yield ownership and permit them to be joined. Its importance derives from its containing the most complete date known until then in all the Americas, written with the system that would later be used on the Maya stelae. This incredibly advanced system shows not only a calculation of time going back almost three thousand years, but also an extraordinary grasp of mathematics since it required a knowledge of the concept of zero, without which it is impossible to write numbers by position. Without this knowledge, even the Romans were limited to simple mathematical operations. Therefore, this invention, always attributed to the Mayas who were more advanced in other matters, should be considered an Olmec achievement.

More than twenty statues in the round of nude men have been recovered, some wearing a breechcloth or a belt and some wearing a collar and helmet. Usually they are seated with their hands resting on their knees or legs but sometimes they have their hands on their chest or at their sides. Some bear objects that appear to be coffers or cylindrical bars. Perhaps the most remarkable, despite its small size, is the "wrestler" of Santa María Uzpanapa, one of the greatest of Olmec works of art. All the different pieces have an obvious unity of style.

Together with this magnificent sculpture are the small carvings in jade and other fine stones. Extremely delicate but within a style unmistakably related to the monolothic statues, it is evident that, although not strictly contemporary, they all come from the same culture. The Olmecs also made numerous ornaments and various objects that are still unique.

Miguel Covarrubias has said: "... Olmec art is distinguished by the simplicity and sensual realism of its forms and by the strength and spontaneity of its concepts. The Olmec artists delighted in representing human beings in thick, solid, chubby shapes. They liked smooth, highly polished surfaces, with lightly incised lines to indicate supplementary features such as tattoos, dress details, ornaments, or glyphs. These lines are precise with an almost geometric style of soft curves and rounded rectangles."

The constant element in all these creations is the jaguar, or rather a combination of man and animal. Just as centuries later the cultures of Nahuatl origin would take the eagle as their symbol, the Olmecs dedicated all their fervor or terror to the jaguar; and it appears everywhere as an animal or as a semihuman character. The intimate association of man and animal was basic to Mesoamerican thought because the *nahual* was the magic belief that individual life was bound to the fate of some animal, which was the *nahual* of that individual. But the animal itself was deified because he was similarly the *nahual* of a god; or the god may also have had his *nahual*, by which he was represented. Thus, the Olmecs had the man-jaguar or the god-jaguar, while Quetzalcoatl in Teotihuacan was the god-bird-serpent, and later Tezcatlipoca would be a god-eagle, which was the sun itself.

The Olmec was especially interested in pathological beings—dwarfs, hunchbacks, the diseased—and in producing artificial deformities in the head or teeth of man. All these ideas would continue and we find them in many parts of Mesoamerica.

The widespread diffusion of Olmec style was probably due to two causes: trade and religion. As stated earlier, the simple agricultural base of the Olmecs could not support such a complex population. From what we know of later cultures and from more concrete evidence, it would seem that trade met this need by bringing in numerous products and exporting others. It is also possible that outside groups attributed the success of the Olmecs to the power of their gods, above all to the jaguar. Therefore, this cult was not only exported but it attracted pilgrimages to the Olmec region to honor the latter's powerful gods.

All this suggests a much more homogeneous society already divided into social classes with specialists who carved stone or jade, constructed monuments, or devoted themselves to trade and perhaps war and religion. Although we know nothing about the Olmec political organization, the area probably did not constitute a single state, but was divided among a series of city-states united in some form among themselves, which did not mean that there were no internal rivalries.

Around 500 B.C. the Olmec region entered a long decline in which it gradually lost its cohesion and preponderant position. But magnificent objects were still produced, isolated survivals of the old splendid civilization; and the most remarkable invention of all, the calendar and the use of zero, was a later contribution. Here, as in other civilizations, the tree bore some of its most beautiful fruit when it was dying.

It is difficult to determine the reasons for the fall of the Olmecs. Possibly other regions had developed sufficiently to undermine their strength; or perhaps their creative leaders had become oppressive, causing popular unrest and situations that ultimately led to the end of this first great Mexican epoch. After the death of the Olmec culture, the region in which it had flowered never recovered its importance, and the center that had radiated culture became only a dim light that no longer illuminated the course of Mesoamerican history.

3

TEOTIHUACAN AND THE URBAN SOCIETY

OUT OF THE RUINS of the Olmec world, a series of related cultures, although each with distinctive features, began to emerge within the Maya region, in Oaxaca and Veracruz, and especially in the mountain valleys of Central Mexico. They were to raise Mesoamerica to its zenith over a period lasting from the start of the Christian Era to the year 900.

Because it would be impossible to deal with all of them in this chapter, we shall attempt to describe only the most powerful one: the Teotihuacan man, who was based in the Valleys of Mexico and Puebla and whose impact is still being felt by the Mexicans of today. Using the culture he had inherited as a foundation, he went on to construct a magnificent edifice, an urban civilization such as had never been seen in the Americas.

But let us begin at the beginning. About four hundred years before Christ there were a number of small scattered hamlets in the area that was later to become a city. Two centuries later these clusters of huts began to merge until together they formed a large sprawling town of some 10,000 inhabitants. By this time, Cuicuilco, which had been the most important ceremonial center of the Valley of Mexico, had disappeared under a lava flow from the volcano, Xitle. People from near and far flocked to the future Teotihuacan to farm its fertile, spring-fed soil and to work in early crafts such as obsidian shaping and polishing, which was becoming more and more profitable.

By the beginning of the Christian Era, Teotihuacan had taken on the form of a city. It covered almost eight square miles and had some fifty thousand inhabitants. There had been much building activity; not only was the Pyramid of the Sun raised to its present height but the interior of the Pyramid of the Moon was completed and at least the northern part of the Avenue of the Dead was laid out. The city's north-south orientation, although a few degrees off, recalls that of La Venta and suggests an ancestral legacy.

With these constructions, Teotihuacan was well on its way to becoming an important religious center. Nearby and ever more distant towns were increasingly drawn into the Teotihuacan orbit. Four centuries after the birth of Christ, Teotihuacan was already a large city for although it still occupied only eight square miles, it had a much higher density of buildings and, therefore, of population.

At that time a political organization appeared, an imperialist state which embarked on a series of conquests or at least commercial incursions as far as Oaxaca and Veracruz and even to Guatemala. It exercised its hegemony over various populations either subdued by military conquest or attracted by the trade and growing prestige of the great city and its presiding gods.

These farflung expeditions were not so much a consequence of the city as of the vast zone around it, dominated by the metropolitan culture, which embraced the Valleys of Mexico and Puebla-Tlaxcala and extended to Tulancingo in Hidalgo and possibly Tehuacan. Teotihuacan thus established a center of action more powerful than any created by its Toltec and Mexica successors. Cholula ensured control of the region and became the second city of the empire, just as Puebla was to become the second city of New Spain during the Viceroyalty.

During this period, the overall plan of the city of Teotihuacan lengthened the Avenue of the Dead two miles to the south and opened avenues to the east and west, thereby forming a cross that divided the city into quadrants. At its center, facing a huge quadrangle (probably the palace) was the temple of Quetzalcoatl. Across the street was the marketplace surrounded by a number of buildings probably used for administration of the city and the empire. The prolongation of the Avenue of the Dead cut across the easiest route between the Valleys of Puebla and Mexico. Thenceforth, travellers and merchants had to traverse the city, giving Teotihuacan tighter control over the Valleys and increasing the volume of its trade.

Among the many buildings of this period was the monumental group of the Pyramid of the Moon—by then completed—and the majestic plaza separating it from the Avenue of the Dead. This plaza, one of the most beautiful in the world, was an extraordinary triumph of Mesoamerican ceremonial architecture. A similar triumph was the sculptured façade of the Temple of Quetzalcoatl.

These and many of the other buildings utilized a new architectural style in which the exterior of the pyramid platform alternated a short *talud* or sloping wall with a *tablero* or rectangular inset panel until the desired height was reached. All the monuments were faced with stone and covered with a coat of stucco on which murals or simply plain colors could be painted. In this way, the stone disappeared completely from view and the drab ruins we see today were for its inhabitants a city full of color. Both interior and exterior frescoes often represented beautiful scenes such as the "mythological animals." Mural painting was so successful as an art form that it continued through the centuries.

This was also the period of great monolithic sculptures like the Goddess of Water, the so-called "Tlaloc," now in front of the National Museum of Anthropology.

The tremendous changes in the city were not confined to public buildings. In many places, the former modest houses were replaced by vast groups of dwellings with roofs of wooden beams and with stone walls covered by plaster and sometimes decorated with merlons. The nature of these dwellings, which were obviously residential, is nonetheless not clear. They have sometimes been called palaces, which would be correct when they served to house a high-ranking person; but in many instances, they were divided into a series of apartments housing various families who were related through blood or simply tribal ties and who had their own temple located within the community.

Some *barrios* (a kind of ward or borough of the city) were defined as much by the occupation of their residents as by their tribal origin. One barrio would produce pottery, another figurines, and another obsidian objects. We know of craft workshops of ceramists, lapidarians, and specialists in such materials as shell, slate, adobe, bricks and stucco. Many others, of course, have vanished without a trace.

The barrios where foreigners lived were especially interesting. A tomb in the style of Monte Albán has been found in the barrio occupied by natives of the Valley of Oaxaca, whereas the Teotihuacan people either buried their dead in graves or—so much the worse for archaeology—cremated them.

Between 350 and 650 years after Christ the city reached its apogee, not with more area but with construction so dense that its inhabitants may have reached a total of 200,000. Although we are accustomed to cities of millions, in the middle of the seventh century the world had only a fraction of today's population and cities were much smaller. As Rome declined, it lost population so rapidly that by the tenth century it had less than 10,000 people. No other city in Europe, with the exception of Constantinople, exceeded 20,000 inhabitants. According to its plans, Changan, the capital of the Tang Empire in China, would have been much larger than Teotihuacan; but probably those plans were never carried out. In any event, Teotihuacan was the most populous city of its time. There was nothing approaching it in Africa or the rest of America.

The size of the city and density of its population required a complex and strong central organization. It would. have been impossible to govern that number of inhabitants and its vast territories with the techniques of a tribal society. Furthermore, Teotihuacan society was composed of different social classes. The lowest classes lived in the barrios and were artisans or market traders who were still united by old family ties and who had owned land in common when they had been farmers. Nevertheless, the barrios of Teotihuacan were far more urban than rural. Several barrios were grouped in each one of the four quadrants of the city, a division that may have been patterned after the earlier tribal organization. The smallest unit was the family that lived in its house or apartment; the second was the barrio that joined together several families; and the third was the four large sectors of the city, each comprising a number of barrios. The social structure was crowned by the imperial society, which held authority, knowledge, and priestly privilege. However, between the imperial society and the barrios were three groups whose position we do not know, but who were quite high on the social scale.

The first group were the merchants, not those who displayed their modest wares on market-day, but those who went off on long expeditions to take and to bring back many different products. Perishable items have disappeared and we find evidence of them only in the murals where we see, for example, cocoa, cotton, and quetzal feathers. Some luxury objects of jade and other fine stones have survived. These powerful merchants may also have collected the tributes imposed on the subject populations.

The second group were the soldiers, who were rarely portrayed, although they must have been very important. It has often been stated that Teotihuacan was a peaceful theocracy governing a state in which war had almost no place. Although war does not seem to have been chronic, as it became later, it is not credible that so powerful a state could have existed without armed defense and could have expanded without recourse to military force. Teotihuacan art contains a few references to war: one fresco depicts armed men, and a series of scenes suggest human sacrifice and the ritual use of blood. In Mesoamerica prisoners of war were the victims most acceptable to the god. The apparent lack of militarism in Teotihuacan could stem from the fact that the warrior and his activities did not have the prestige they were to acquire later. Victories were attributed to the priests, since battles were won by the gods.

The third and most important group were the priests. In addition to their religious functions, they possessed the highest culture and knowledge. They planned the buildings and indicated the days for celebrations and ceremonies. They kept the calendar in order and measured time, for which they had to be experts in astronomy and mathematics. Probably they alone knew how to write and they were in charge of directing the great mural compositions, which therefore were almost always related to religious themes. And religion was the center of everything. People came to Teotihuacan from near and far not only to trade but because they were attracted by its majesty. The city was the basis of the aesthetic and emotional appeal exercised for so long by the Teotihuacan religion. Pilgrims came to ask favors of the all-powerful gods who had made such grandeur possible and, like the tourists of today, they contributed to the city's prosperity.

There is no question that Teotihuacan was a truly urban society, divided into social classes and professional groups, having a complex economy, and ruled by a political state, even if we do not know how it was formed. This means that we are dealing with a complete civilization.

Between 650 and 700 A.D., Teotihuacan was invaded, set to the torch, plundered, and in part deliberately destroyed. Signs of the final fire are clear in many of the temples along the Avenue of the Dead and especially in that splendid priestly palace, Quetzal-papalotl. Here, the invader, not satisfied with burning its roof, also tore down its magnificent columns carved with the god's image and buried the stones in an open pit in the patio. Similarly, he ripped out the great stones of the steps of the Pyramid of the Moon—now replaced in their original site—and scattered them about the plaza. Many of the valuable offerings that had been placed in front of the temples during their construction were looted, so that now there are only empty boxes.

The sack of this mighty city did it more damage than its subsequent thirteen centuries of being abandoned to nature and to human pillage. We know neither the reasons for this event which shook Mesoamerica, nor who carried out the attack, nor how it could have happened. It is evident that during the last years of its glory, Teotihuacan began to lose part—and the most important part—of its metropolitan zone, when the Valley of Puebla was conquered by a new people. Its ties with more distant places also began to diminish or disappear.

It is possible that the internal weakening of the city—without which its collapse seems inexplicable—was due to the fact that several different groups lived there and some may have resented being subordinate to others. But there is evidence that the principal cause may have originated in the excessive centralization of power in the city, which drove the populace to rebel against its governors. The latter, representing the gods on earth, had changed from a creative to an oppressive minority. These priests, who at first had given an enormous impulse to culture and to material progress and had achieved marvellous works of art, thought only of retaining their power once they had triumphed. Their rigidity and lack of inner strength made them fall easy victims to the first people who dared to attack the city. These audacious warriors might have been the Otomí, who lived to the north and northeast of the city. No longer nomads, their long contact with Mesoamerica had raised their culture to a level where they were strong enough to conquer a nation as powerful and organized as Teotihuacan.

Much has been said about natural causes such as environmental changes that produced a drier climate, thereby limiting agricultural possibilities. This is not likely, although the continual cutting down of trees through many centuries had deforested the hills leaving them eroded and barren.

Whatever the motives and agents of the disaster, the fact is that Teotihuacan died and with it, its great culture. But it left an immense legacy whose influence is still felt and whose legend barely ended with the Spanish conquest.

The fall of Teotihuacan began a chain reaction that precipitated the end of Monte Albán and of all the great Maya centers in the course of the ninth century. Many of the inhabitants of Teotihuacan emigrated to other places, taking with them their culture and founding new towns. Those who remained must have mixed with the conquerors, who installed themselves in the ruins in adobe houses with mud floors. From this cultural mixture was to emerge the new period of Mexican history that we call the Toltec. The recent arrivals took from Teotihuacan many cultural features that would be passed on to the Mexicas and, in a way very characteristic of Mesoamerica, they began to feel themselves to be not only the descendants but also representatives of this glorious past.

Thus, history was turned into myth, into a legendary past in which the great city had not been created by men but by giants and the gods themselves; this explained the name given to the monumental ruins. Teotihuacan means place of the gods or place where gods are made. The legend of the Fifth Sun relates part of this process of deification.

According to the legend, Teotihuacan existed in the era of the Fourth Sun (the three preceding Suns had already perished). With the death of Teotihuacan and, thence, the death of man, the gods were in despair because there was no one left to pay them honor. Having gathered together in Teotihuacan, one of them was changed into the Sun and another into the Moon, and these are the gods of our historical era who still shine upon us. This legend explains why Moctezuma II made a pilgrimage every year to Teotihuacan and why he ordered a temple to be built near the Pyramid of the Sun. He wanted to venerate those unknown but powerful Teotihuacan gods.

Even in its decadence, Teotihuacan continued to be an eagerly sought-after prize until at least the beginning of the colonial period; and the lords of Texcoco were proud to possess it. As the first urban and really civilized society that existed in what is now Mexico, its prestige was well deserved. The indigenous civilization of the highland was formed with Teotihuacan and this is what we have inherited and what has become Mexican. Without its triumph we ourselves would not live over seven thousand feet above sea level in a region that since Teotihuacan has become the geopolitical center of the world called Anáhuac by the Mexicas.

4

THE END OF THE INDIAN WORLD

THE TOLTEC SUCCESSORS to Teotihuacan created an empire that lasted some three centuries. Its collapse in turn gave rise to a number of states small and large that were permanently at war with one another, a situation that lasted until the close of the fifteenth century. Among them lived an insignificant group which we mistakenly call Aztec, although its name should be Mexica. The Mexicas had arrived with the immigrants who poured in from different regions and destroyed the Toltec Empire, establishing themselves on its ruins. Around the second half of the thirteenth century the Mexicas entered the Valley of Mexico where practically all the land was occupied by nations partly descended from the Teotihuacans and partly formed by the new arrivals.

In 1276 the Mexicas settled in Chapultepec, where they remained for some time until they were defeated in a terrible battle and taken as prisoners to Culhuacan, governed by a dynasty of Toltec descent. The Culhuas gave land near Tizapán to the Mexicas in the hope that they would be destroyed by the huge number of serpents infesting the region. But with the irony typical of Mexican history, the chronicle relates that the Mexicas were delighted to see the serpents and ate them with pleasure.

In 1325 they moved to a small island which was part of an archipelago in Lake Texcoco and which would eventually become the city of Tenochtitlan. Settling there indicated not only their poverty but also their faith, courage, and tenacity. Precisely because the island was so unattractive, it had never been permanently occupied and did not belong to any of the neighboring kingdoms. Nevertheless, for some time the Mexicas had to be vassals of the most important power of that period, the Tepanecas of Azcapotzalco.

By 1376 the Mexicas had a real monarchy, descended, through Culhuacan, from the royal house of the Toltecs; and this monarchy became more important with the passage of time. The fourth king, Itzcoatl, who governed from 1427 to 1440, made an alliance with other powers and conquered the Tepanecas. From that moment, and for the first time, the Mexicas were completely independent and ready to embark on an imperial career. The actual founder of the empire was Moctezuma I, who reigned until 1469. Thanks to his military talents, his victorious campaigns had carried him to what is today the center of Veracruz and to the Mixtec region of Oaxaca. But Moctezuma was more than just a great conqueror; he was also the organizer of a new state, a builder, and a patron of the arts. He brought in eminent architects from Chalco to construct his city as well as famous goldsmiths from the Mixteca to fashion the splendid jewelry that was to amaze Europe in the sixteenth century. The older huts were replaced by stone buildings in accordance with an overall design.

His three successors, who vastly expanded the empire to at least the frontier of present-day Guatemala, were followed in 1502 by Moctezuma II. The new emperor could feel proud of his family and his people. In fifteen generations, the once miserable and rejected tribe had become the head of the Anáhuac, "the circle of the world between the seas." Moctezuma knew that it was all the gift of the mighty god Huitzilopochtli, who had fulfilled his old but not forgotten prophecy: "I shall make you lords and kings of whatever there is in the world, wherever it may be, and you will have innumerable and endless vassals that will pay you tribute ... and you will see all this, for this is my true task and I was sent here for this." Although Moctezuma actually ruled an empire the size of modern Italy, composed of various regions and climates and inhabited by people who spoke many languages, Mexica trade and influence extended still farther. Moctezuma presided over a sumptuous court. He had been a valiant warrior, and he was the High Priest of Huitzilopochtli. But his most notable qualities—his refinement, generosity, and fatalis—were the cause of his indecision and weakness in dealing with Cortés and were what doomed him and his empire.

The moment to study Tenochtitlan with some hope of understanding it is precisely on the eve of its fall. The descriptions of the conquistadors and other documents as well as archaeological findings present a fascinating, if incomplete, picture of the life of this last Indian capital, product of two thousand years of urban life in Mesoamerica. It has been considered almost a miracle that in less than a century a small wandering tribe should have created this city with a highly developed urban pattern. Actually, in the light of what went before, it was no miracle. The Aztecs were heirs to an ancient tradition going back through the Toltec Tula and its successors to the urban pattern of Teotihuacan, where the first civilization in the highland had emerged.

Tenochtitlan-Tlatelolco—that is, the combination of two islands referred to simply as Tenochtitlan, which was the main one—occupied an area of almost five square miles in 1519. The original islands were smaller, but they had been added to by mud scooped up from the marshy borders of the lake. On the basis of its area and the amount of tributes collected by the Empire, it is estimated that in 1521 Tenochtitlan could not have had more than 80,000 inhabitants. Although these figures may seem very low today, at the beginning of the sixteenth century only four European cities—Paris, Naples, Venice, and Milan—had just over 100,000 inhabitants each. The largest city in Spain, Seville, had a population of 45,000 according to a 1530 census. It is therefore not strange that Tenochtitlan appeared enormous to the Spanish conquistadors.

Apart from its size, this American Venice was truly impressive. On all sides rose pyramids topped with high temples, and towering over the rest was the Great Temple. The entire city had a pyramidal profile with the Great Temple as both axis and peak. Palaces and then houses diminished in size going toward the shores of the lake which were bordered with fertile *chinampas* (man-made islands) covered with flowers and vegetables. All around was water with other islands, and their many cities seemed to weave a crown about the capital.

This was the spectacle described by Bernal Díaz del Castillo: "... and when we saw so many cities and populated valleys in the water and other great towns on dry land and that straight level causeway leading to Mexico, we were amazed and said that it was like the enchantments told of in the legends of Amadís because of the lofty towers and buildings, all of masonry, rising from the water. Some of our soldiers even said that it must be all a dream. It is not surprising that I write in this way because there is so much to think about that I do not know how to describe it, seeing things never heard of or even dreamed about."

The symmetry and planning admired by the conquistadors (it should be recalled that medieval cities had little of this) originated in the Aztec political and social organization, with its division into four parts. The city was therefore divided into four barrios (Tlatelolco was a fifth barrio added after its annexation to the city). Each *calpulli* or barrio contained various subdivisions; they were really the remains of the old clan associations which became subordinate to the imperial state. The four original *calpullis* of the city, once they were geographically established, met at a central point which was the area occupied by the Great Temple, the imperial palaces, and the palaces of the ranking lords. The Temple enclosure had four doors, recalling the four barrios, each one oriented toward one of the cardinal points. From each door emerged a causeway that marked the boundaries of the *calpullis*. Thus, Tenochtitlan was a very orderly city laid out as a quadrangle, actually similar to the way it would later be organized by the Spaniards. Even the natural irregularity of the borders of the island had been modified by the rectangular *chinampas* that had been gradually constructed to expand the habitable area.

All this was evidence that the growth of Tenochtitlan was carefully planned, with nothing left to chance. There was even a special official, the *calmimilolcatl*, who made sure that houses were properly lined along the straight streets and canals. Although many streets were actually canals that could be travelled only in canoes, footpaths almost always ran along their banks. Wherever a canal crossed a causeway or another canal, there was a bridge of strong planks that could easily be removed in case of danger; and this was precisely what caused the rout of Cortés on the day of the *Noche Triste* (Night of Sorrow).

Its natural setting of canals and surrounding lakes (as was true of the colonial city and even of independent Mexico until very recently) meant that Tenochtitlan would be flooded every time the level of the lakes rose. Huge walls—called *albarradones* by the Spaniards—were built to contain the lakes within their banks as well as to separate fresh from salt water. The principal engineering project, said to have been directed by Netzahualcoyotl, managed to prevent at least major floods. There were also public employees like the *acolnahuacatl* who patrolled the borders of the island to make sure that water filtering into newly built *chinampas* would not cause them to crumble into the lake. Nevertheless, the problem was of such magnitude that neither the Indian technicians nor three centuries of colonial rule could solve it; only now is there adequate flood control.

Tenochtitlan had drinkable spring water, but not enough, and two aqueducts were constructed to bring additional water from the mainland. One, ordered by Moctezuma I, went to Chapultepec and a later one was built to Coyoacan by Ahuitzotl. The one to Chapultepec was a more ambitious work consisting of two parallel channels so that when one was being repaired, the other could remain in use. As long as Tenochtitlan retained control of these springs, its population was assured a supply of fresh water.

The major part of labor and art was naturally dedicated to the temples, of which there were many in Tenochtitlan. The chief ones were Tlatelolco and the Great Temple in the center of the city. According to Sahagún, the latter included seventy-eight buildings surrounded by a wall decorated with the famous Coatepantli serpents inherited from Tula. The tallest pyramid honored the gods Tlaloc and Huitzilopochtli. Many other temples were within the enclosure as well as the ball-court and the *Calmecac*, where the sons of noblemen studied.

The nobility and other authorities lived in high-roofed rooms arranged around one or several square patios. There could be as many as fifty apartments, but no matter how large the building, there were no windows and only one door to the street. Life was led within the complex and the apartments received light only through the doors that opened into the interior patios. Often a small temple would be erected in the principal patio for the private devotions of those living there. The buildings were kept dry by an excellent drainage system. These more important houses were constructed entirely of masonry and their flat roofs, very different from the inclined ones of the temples, were decorated with merlons. On the roof, which formed a terrace, restful hours could be spent watching the sunset or perhaps the stars on the rare warm nights of the highland. Houses were of one story but there were cases of additional stories built on the terrace. The walls were covered with painted stucco to make them waterproof and to give them a finer finish.

On the outskirts of the city, where the common people lived, each house was surrounded by a little garden where flowers—so loved by the Aztecs—would be cultivated as well as useful plants. These more modest homes had foundations made of stone; their adobe walls supported a flat roof of beams. Generally, one rectangular room sufficed to lodge an entire family, for the kitchen, granary, and bathhouse were separately installed in the garden. An Indian house could no more be without a canoe at its door than today's North American house can be without an automobile in its garage. Every house in Tenochtitlan seems to have had one and even two canoes, since it was the sole means of transport not only through the canals but also to cross the lake. The canoes were varied, some plain and simple, others decorated and with carved prows.

An outline of the economic history of Tenochtitlan reflects the political and military events of the city. For example, toward the end of the fourteenth century there were still very few feathers in the market and these were of inferior quality. The clothing sold then was of maguey fiber. Small jades and turquoise stones as well as cotton clothing for men appeared at the beginning of the fifteenth century. This occurred precisely when Huitzilihuitl was winning battles in Morelos, which was then a producer of cotton.

In 1430 came the victory over Azcapotzalco and from that time on there was a profusion of feathers of the quetzal and other rare birds, jaguar skins, jades, turquoise, and gold jewelry. According to a chronicle of 1450, "these things abound" as well as cloth embroidered with feathers for nobles and embroidered skirts and *huipiles* (a sleeveless overblouse) for women. The great luxury of drinking chocolate began around that time; the cacao beans also served as currency.

The wars of Ahuizotl brought new products: huge feather head-dresses; insignia of mosaics and feathers; all kinds of animal skins; larger pieces of jewelry in new forms; shields of mosaic and turquoise; and finely woven cloth, embroidered or dyed in exotic colors. The wealthy could adorn themselves with strips of paper or rabbit fur and they carried fans of guacamaya feathers with handles of gold. They drank their chocolate from lacquered gourds and they ate with tortoise-shell spoons. Besides these luxury articles, which could only be bought by the nobility of Tenochtitlan, the market offered innumerable products obtained through tribute or brought by nearby traders for the everyday use of the average citizen.

In the light of the long list of items displayed, it is not surprising that the market was a very special attraction not only as a trading center but for many other reasons. People came from all over to buy, to eat, and to sell; they also came to entertain themselves, to arrange business matters, to make offerings to the gods, to catch up on the news, and to greet friends. The market was the social center—the "newspaper" of Tenochtitlan which reported the events, the edicts, and the religious festivals. Sometimes as many as 60,000 people gathered in this immense human anthill, a clear indication of the commercial supremacy of Tenochtitlan.

At the hub of all this activity were the great merchants who organized caravans to the limits of their world and who brought in and took out merchandise. They were so important to the material spirit of Tenochtitlan that they were treated as petty nobility. Ahuizotl, for example, had permitted them to use on certain occasions the insignia reserved to the aristocracy. Nevertheless, the life of these merchants, who were the wealthiest group in the Indian city, was not free of the difficulties that so often beset the economically powerful. One chronicle reports an amusing detail: "the emperor sometimes lost his love for them and used their revenues to support his luxury and pomp."

The Aztec nobility, which was such a small group in the times of Izcoatl, began to grow. It had its own estates and special privileges. The continual expansion of the aristocracy undoubtedly diminished the importance of the tribal organizations—the *calpullis*—which comprised the common people. Two careers, the army and the priesthood, were open to the noble; but they were not mutually exclusive. This dual role of the nobility gave the Aztec state its character of theocratic militarism. The warrior was the arm, perhaps the head; the priest was the soul. Military leaders shared the glory and the booty of the victories, they used the conquered people to work their lands as well as to obtain a broad assortment of products, and they enjoyed enormous prestige. These men with "hearts of stone" were the ones who were idealized by the Aztec world.

But the priest possessed the mightiest weapon: he was the earthly representative of god. And just as the *calpulli* became subordinate to the empire, the priest was no longer the tribal magician but part of an organized body of religious professionals with a hierarchy and specialized functions. They were in charge of the Great Temple; they belonged to the imperial society; and they had their own income from conquered territories and of course from the offerings of the faithful. Another source of priestly power was culture. The priest was the repository of almost all the knowledge of Tenochtitlan: medicine, astronomy, calendaric calculations, writing, history, literature, and philosophy. In the school of the nobles, the *Calmecac*, besides all these subjects the priests taught law, government, and military strategy. Therefore, the graduate of the *Calmecac* had been trained to reach the highest posts, which were beyond the modest education received by the son of the *macehual* (commoner) in the tribal schools.

Above everyone was the emperor, the undisputed sovereign, high priest of Huitzilopochtli, supreme military commander. His position was not hereditary, but elective, although from the time of Acamipichtli he had always been chosen from the same family. After Izcoatl and especially after the death of Nezahualcoyotl of Texcoco, the emperors had cleverly maneuvered to place the ruler of Mexico above the other two kings of the Triple Alliance. By the time Moctezuma II came to power neither of his allies even attempted to be his equal. In fact, he imposed the candidates he wanted on the thrones of Texcoco and Tacuba. This man had everything his world could offer: many wives, servants, games, dwarfs, hunchbacks, poets, actors, and musicians to amuse him, as well as the veneration of his subjects who almost deified him. His court rivalled the Asiatic in splendor and despotism and it had been established much earlier. It is remarkable that the imperial family had not reached the point of decadence. Moctezuma II was a valiant warrior and a dedicated priest, although, unlike his ancestors who had been basically men of action, he was thoughtful and contemplative, qualities he may have inherited from his illustrious grandfather, Nezahualcoyotl.

However, the grandeur of Tenochtitlan could not be explained either by political ability, or the economy, or geography. It was their religion, their messianic mission, their belief in their destiny that made the Aztecs different from the tribes around them. Their vision of the world was based on their profound belief in the promise of Huitzilopochtli which gave them the certainty that, ever since the deepest roots of their obscure past, they were a chosen people. In their days of misfortune they had paid with infinite suffering for the promise of a glorious future. In their days of triumph they had to go on bearing the terrible burden of keeping their god, the sun, alive. Every evening, as the sun sank behind the mountains to the west, came the terrible doubt: Would it reappear tomorrow? During the night would it defeat its enemies, be able to fight off the tigers and other terrors that would attack it? To assure its victory over its enemies, it must be given strength. Unfortunately for the neighbors of the Aztecs, the only nourishment acceptable to the sun was human blood. Therefore, blood became indispensable to the survival of the world.

The most elementary instinct of self-preservation and the most obvious self-interest indicated that such blood should be obtained by sacrificing people other than the Aztecs. After all, the Aztecs not only saved themselves but also the rest of the world; not only was the sun for them, it also illuminated others. So even the rite that appeared most cruel could be logically justified. Because the blood of conquered warriors was most valuable, war became necessary not only as an economic but also as a religious factor. As the Aztecs gathered more and more conquests and victories, Huitzilopochtli should have been satisfied with the torrents of foreign blood poured out in his honor. But by then he was so powerful and his temple so elevated that he no longer gave advice to his people; he accepted only veneration. After the fifteenth century the terrible voice of the god disappeared from the chronicles and he never again spoke a word.

In his temple on high, the divinity was represented by an enormous statue shaped of *masa* (a kind of paste made from ground corn) in which jewels were set. In his left hand he held a *xiuhcoatl*, the fire serpent, the divine weapon that assured the triumph of the Aztec armies forever. Huitzilopochtli had been born grasping the serpent and with it he had eliminated all his enemies. Thus, in the final days of the siege of Tenochtitlan, when all seemed lost, the emperor as a last resort gave to a young warrior the invincible weapon of Huitzilopochtli with which to enter combat and annihilate the Spaniards. The failure of this attempt ended the war. The Spaniards with their allies, says the Texcocan chronicle, "climbed the tower and threw down the idols, especially in the main chapel of Huitzilopochtli. Cortés and Ixtlixochitl arrived at the same time and they both rushed on the statue, Cortés to tear off its gold mask and Ixtlixochitl to cut off the head of the one he had so recently worshipped as his god."

Bibliography

BERNAL, Ignacio. *Mexico Before Cortez: Art, History, Legend.* Translated by Willie Barnstone. Garden City, New York, Anchor Books, Anchor Press/Doubleday, 1975.

CLAVIGERO, Francisco Saverio. *The History of Mexico.* New York, Garland Publishers, 1979.

DAVIES, Nigel. *The Aztecs: A History.* Norman, University of Oklahoma Press, 1980.

FOSTER, Elizabeth Andros, trans. and ed. *Motolinia's History of the Indians of New Spain.* Westport, Conn., Greenwood Press, 1973.

GRAHAM, John A., ed. *Ancient Mesoamerica: Selected Readings.* Palo Alto, California, Peek Publications, 1966.

MORLEY, Sylvanus. *The Ancient Maya.* Stanford, California, Stanford University Press, 1958.

SAHAGÚN, Fray Bernardino de. *The War of Conquest. How It Was Waged Here in Mexico.* Translated by Arthur J. O. Anderson and Charles E. Dibble. Salt Lake City, University of Utah Press, 1978.

———. *The Florentine Codex: General History of the Things of New Spain. Book 8, Kings and Lords.* Translated by Charles E. Dibble and Arthur J. O. Anderson. Santa Fe, New Mexico, University of Utah and the School of American Research, 1979.

SANDERS, William and Barbara PRICE. *Mesoamerica: The Evolution of a Civilization.* New York, Random House, 1968.

SOUSTELLE, Jacques. *Daily life of the Aztecs on the Eve of the Spanish Conquest.* Translated by Patrick O'Brien. Stanford, California, Stanford University Press, 1976.

THOMPSON, J. Eric S. *The Rise and Fall of Mayan Civilization.* Norman, University of Oklahoma Press, 1954.

WOLF, Eric. *Sons of the Shaking Earth.* Chicago, University of Chicago Press, 1959.

II. THE VICEROYALTY

Alejandra Moreno Toscano

1

THE CENTURY OF CONQUEST

In Mexican history, the sixteenth century was the Century of Conquest. This name encompassed not only the military event itself, but also the long period of adjustment that led, not without violence, to a new situation, the Colony.

The Century of Conquest was divided into two different periods. In the first, which extended from 1519 to more or less the middle of the century, the private interests of the conquistadors triumphed over the Indian world, soon to be subjected to systematic exploitation. This dominance of private interests can be explained by various circumstances. The Spanish Crown had to resort to private individuals to support and conduct the explorations of discovery and conquest of the New World because it did not have the financial resources to do so. Even the voyage of Columbus was financed by the Catholic Queen Isabella as a private enterprise (according to tradition, she pawned her personal jewels to raise the necessary money) and therefore the land discovered was considered from that time to be the exclusive patrimony of the Crown of Castille.

In order to attract the private funds needed to cover the expenses of such expeditions and at the same time to keep the newly discovered lands under dominion of the Crown, an agreement was worked out whereby the Crown granted to private parties certain rights in the conquest and exploitation of the territories in exchange for recognition of its sovereignty and "a fifth" of the resulting revenues. This system of private enterprise made it possible to organize the discovery and conquest and it also explained why the conquistadors were so anxious to recoup their expenses and reward their efforts at the expense of the Indians. Furthermore, because the conquests were almost always unpredictable— Columbus never suspected that he had discovered a new continent and, until the arrival of Cortés in Mexico, no one could have imagined the wealth it contained—the conquistadors made their decisions as they went along and the Crown later accepted these decisions as accomplished facts.

The conquistadors received as "reward" for their conquests a certain number of Indian servants, tributes, *encomiendas*, and grants of land or urban lots in proportion to the initial contribution they had made in arms and horses to the enterprise; but the proportion of this "reward" was fixed by the conquistadors themselves. This meant that at the beginning the conquistadors used and abused their rights without any control, paying no heed to the orders issued over and over by the Crown against mistreatment of the Indians. This early state of affairs gradually changed as the Crown and its representatives managed to centralize in their hands the functions of the organization of the new society.

The latter part of the century was characterized precisely by the opposite tendency: increased royal participation in making decisions, greater control of the abuses of the conquistadors, and the emergence of a deliberate policy of legal protection for the Indian.

In the early years of Spanish-Indian contact, the principal conflict was between the old pre-Columbian society and the new state of affairs as embodied by the conquistador. Perhaps the figure of the conquistador dominated the sixteenth century because some of the best histories of the Conquest were written by historians of the romantic school who found in him a model that combined the personal attributes of individual action, free will, and triumph over adversity. And in the Indian world they found everything picturesque and colorful needed for a good romantic story. But it is also the conquistador, or rather several conquistadors whose names we can easily remember, who shaped the sixteenth century for other reasons.

Even though more than two thousand individuals risked their lives in the conquest of Tenochtitlan as members of the original expedition of Cortés or as followers of Narváez and Garay, very few benefitted from exploitation of the conquered world. Barely 4 percent of these enriched themselves from the Conquest and they are the ones whose names we recall—Captain Cortés, the two Ávila brothers, Nuño de Guzmán, Vázquez de Tapia, and Diego de Ordaz—and who represent the image of the sixteenth-century Spanish conquistador. The rest ended up repeating in America the trades of their fathers as shoemakers, ironmongers, and carpenters. In writing his history of the Conquest, Bernal Díaz del Castillo portrayed these men—participants but not beneficiaries—and protested against the inequitable distribution of profits.

Because the figure of Cortés loomed large in the first years of colonial history, our histories describe his incredible feats and the havoc he created—from the massacre of Cholula to the siege of Tenochtitlan. Furthermore, the dramatic spectacle of the fall of Tenochtitlan, because of its importance as the center of the Aztec Empire, has helped make the Conquest known only in terms of Cortés and of the Defenders of Tenochtitlan. Much has been written for and against Cortés and Cuauhtémoc, but little on the process of the military struggle, the confrontation of two concepts of warfare, and the expression of conflicts of power and opinion within the ruling Indian group.

It is possible to distinguish broadly several stages in the military conquest. The first, which can be called the "Antillean," was directed by the trade interests and projects of Diego Velázquez, governor of Cuba, and it ended with the founding of Villa Rica (Veracruz) by Cortés on the Gulf coast. Once this city was established in accordance with the ancient Spanish municipal tradition, Cortés had himself elected Captain-General by the *ayuntamiento* (town council) composed of his own men. Cortés could then assume full authority and disavow Velázquez, whose subordinate he had been. Another stage began with the march of Cortés into the interior until his alliance with Tlaxcala. Having observed the differences separating the Indian nations from each other and from the center of the Empire, Cortés realized that he could ally himself with the Tlaxcalans against the Mexicas. The third stage was the entrance of Cortés into the Valley of Mexico and his reception by Moctezuma. Cortés then had the opportunity to see the city and become acquainted with the mechanism of the Empire. When he left the city of Tenochtitlan to confront Pánfilo de Narváez, the Mexicas rose up against the Spaniards and, on the return of Cortés, the conquistadors had to remain shut up in the palace where they were holding Moctezuma hostage. During the episode known as the *Noche Triste*, the Aztecs drove the Spaniards from the city. The last phase of this history, the siege and fall of Tenochtitlan, covered the return of Cortés from Tlaxcalan territory, where he had rested with his men, up to the imprisonment of Cuauhtémoc.

The history of the Conquest is well known chronologically and from many different points of view; nonetheless, we still do not know much about the processes that explain it. Nor do we have recent studies of the regional conquests of the interior of the country. If these campaigns seem to be confused in dates and information, it is only because they were carried out rapidly and simultaneously. The initial direction of the regional conquests toward Coatzacoalcos or Pánuco was an attempt to establish strategic points linking the Spanish possessions in the West Indies and Spain. Subsequent incursions into Colima and Zacatula in the west and the subjugation of the Tututepec and Zapotec kingdoms were dictated by the need for a port on the Pacific from which to embark for the Orient. The Spaniards still cherished the idea that they could reach India and China by following the western route, the same route that had brought a Genoese navigator to American soil. A study of the regional conquests is indispensable to understand the mechanisms by which the territory was subdued and to see, as in the negative of a photograph, the degree of political cohesion in the old Aztec Empire.

Before 1521, Cortés had sent several of his captains to form alliances or dominate militarily sites in the interior in order to ensure his victory over the Mexicas. Some centers resisted so fiercely that they were totally destroyed by the conquistadors; but many populations immediately entered into alliances with the Spaniards and, in proof of their support, sent men to fight with the armies of Cortés. If we are to believe Cortés, the siege of Tenochtitlan was conducted by one thousand Spaniards supported by fifty thousand Indian allies. It should be remembered that the expansion of the Aztec Empire had begun under the reign of Izcoatl around 1420, coinciding precisely with the first Portuguese and Spanish explorations in the Atlantic. By 1500 the Mexicas had reached the geographical limits of their empire and when the Spaniards arrived in 1519, barely a generation separated many of the Indian nations from their former condition of independence. For this reason, many of these people regarded Moctezuma as a tyrant and they saw in the Spaniards a possibility of freeing themselves from the Aztec yoke.

Although the sixteenth century was one of military struggle, it was also the beginning of structures that would continue through the colonial period. After their victory, the way in which the conquistadors divided the wealth of the new land, their subjugation of the population first by slavery and later through *encomienda*, and the distribution of land to them by royal grants—all marked the outlines of the new colonial society and established the imbalance between the Spanish and Indian worlds. The dream of the conquistadors, which was to maintain their "conquest"—that is, their status of almost feudal lords in a society organized for their benefit—ended about the middle of the century. As the Spanish Crown began to take control of the situation, it centralized political decision and displaced the old conquistadors from their privileged positions. When the conquistadors realized that they were losing ground, they tried rebellion as a last resort. But the Spanish Crown uncovered the plot of Martín Cortés and executed the two Ávila brothers as its chief conspirators in the main square of Mexico City. The Spanish Crown thus ended the society of the conquistadors and launched the beginning of the new colonial society.

2

THE SPIRITUAL CONQUEST

THE TERM "SPIRITUAL CONQUEST" was coined by Robert Ricard in one
of the classic histories of Mexico. In the process of Christianizing
and Hispanicizing the Indians during the sixteenth century, Ricard
saw the expression of a crisis of conscience, the opportunity to
reinterpret man's condition. The problem of turning the Indian
into a Christian and a Spaniard—in other words, his "westernization"—was also linked to the need to justify the expansion of the
European Empire. Did Spain have the right to place new territories
under its dominion and was the war of conquest a just war? These
were the questions, with conflicting answers, underlying all the
colonizing actions of Spain in America.

Within the Christian tradition of the West, it seemed only right
that a Christian prince should have reconquered the territories that
had been lost in battles against the infidel Moors, since the latters'
claim was illegitimate. But the American Indians were considered
heathens rather than infidels; and as heathens, by natural law they
were in legitimate possession of their land. On the other hand, if they
were barbarians then, according to Aristotle, they were slaves by
nature and their subjugation was not only just but necessary. But if
they were granted to be on an equal plane with Christians, with the
same rights and obligations, then colonial domination would be
condemned. During the early years of the Conquest, these ideas were
continually debated; but as those who justified the expansion of the
western empires gained power and influence, and as the "colonial"

52

condition of the inhabitants of the New World acquired "legality," these questions were no longer asked.

In the same way that the military conquest may be divided into two different periods up to the middle of the sixteenth century, the spiritual conquest passed through two distinct phases beginning with the arrival of the first Franciscan mission in 1523. Its second phase covered the years after 1555 when the First Mexican Council met and defined the situation that was to prevail during the rest of the colonial epoch.

The first phase was characterized by more freedom and independence in the work of the missionaries. Various methods of conversion were tried and new institutions were set up in response to the specific problem of converting the Indian. At that time, missionaries concentrated on the education of young Indians to be sent out to convert and westernize their own world. It was accepted that if the Indian could receive the sacraments, he could also give them and he was therefore trained to exercise priestly functions. In those early years, the basic Christian texts were translated into the vernacular, which was studied and preserved. In brief, it was believed that the purity of primitive Christianity, which had been corrupted in Europe, could be recovered among the Indians. America and specifically the Indian world appeared to the first missionaries as the ideal material for realizing the utopias dreamed of in old Europe.

During the second phase, after the middle of the century, these early premises were radically redefined. For the sake of orthodoxy, the freedom to act and to create institutions enjoyed by the first missionaries was systematically and progressively limited. In the same way that decisions became increasingly centralized in the Spanish Crown, the actions of religious orders were increasingly subject to the authority of the bishops. Many of the institutions that flowered at the beginning of the sixteenth century disappeared when they no longer received official support. It was decided that Indians were not capable of advanced studies for the priesthood and that, instead of keeping their languages alive, they should learn Spanish.

This change in attitude has to be understood in the context of the situation in Europe. It should be remembered that by the middle of the century, when Phillip II came to the throne, Spain had become the defender of a Christian orthodoxy threatened by the Lutheran schism. Furthermore, the Conquest itself had evolved so that by the middle of the century, the main structures of colonial domination were established. The Christianization and Hispanization of the Indian had become a function of the state, which in turn depended on the metropolitan country. The spiritual organization, like the social, would be polarized into the Spanish and Indian worlds.

In this sense, the spiritual conquest was less a crisis of conscience than an integral part of the process of colonial domination in the sixteenth century. It was in many ways much more radical and violent than the military conquest. The military conquistadors maintained, with some modifications, various autochthonous social and power structures such as the *calpulli*, the tribute, and certain collective forms of personal service. On the other hand, the spiritual conquistadors, the missionaries, in order to construct Christianity were determined to destroy all pre-Hispanic spiritual relations in a world that had been based on a religious concept of life. With this, westernization was assured and the old cultures began to disappear.

The challenge of mass conversion of the Indians and thereby justification of the Conquest engendered new institutions and the application of methods and techniques unknown in the West. Many of these procedures and institutions came from the observation and study of such pre-Hispanic activities as teaching (and converting) through the use of the audiovisual capacities of the individual. The Mexican Indians had developed a type of pictograph writing that associated a visual image with a body of knowledge. The religious paintings hung in the early Mexican churches were conceived of less as ornament than as an effective evangelical tool. The missionary would stop in front of each one to explain the image and the symbolism he wanted to convey to the recently converted.

The need for wholesale conversion led the missionaries to incorporate into the design of religious constructions a new and original architectural element, the open chapel. In these chapels, of which a few beautiful examples survive, mass could be celebrated in the huge forecourt of the monasteries before many more people than could have gathered inside the church. This same need also led the missionaries of the sixteenth century to revive certain practices of early Christianity already forgotten in the West, such as baptism by immersion. One of these enormous baptismal fonts still exists today in the monastery of Tzintzuntzan, Michoacán.

The relationship between the old pre-Hispanic institutions of education and the institutions created by the missionaries in the sixteenth century is now being investigated. The schools for Indian nobles and commoners, the *Calmecac* and *Tepuzcalli*, had as their counterparts in the first colonial period the great colleges of Santa Cruz in Santiago Tlatelolco and San José de los Naturales in the monastery of San Francisco, the parochial schools, and the schools of the colonial barrios.

The missionaries studied pre-Hispanic languages and customs in order to show how opposed the old religious practices were to Christianity. Therefore, the spiritual conquest was directly tied to the birth of ethnographic studies in the New World. In the early part of the sixteenth century Spanish missionaries were extremely interested in the Indian languages, many of which they put into writing. They analyzed the internal structure of the principal languages and collected important vocabularies with the precise definitions and different meanings of each word. Furthermore, they translated many religious works into the Indian languages which, thanks to the printing press, they were able to reproduce and circulate among their converts.

Many detailed studies of the religious customs, ceremonies, and practices of the Indians were also made. The most important of these was unquestionably the work carried out by Bernardino de Sahagún, who for ten years patiently collected information from the Indians. From this information the Franciscan friar produced a complete history of the life and religion of the Mexicans which was to permit later scholars to reconstruct aspects of Indian life that otherwise would have been lost forever.

Like the military conquest, the spiritual conquest differed from region to region, generally according to when the various religious orders had entered the territory. The Franciscans, who were the first to arrive, established themselves in the center of Mexico and some parts of Michoacán, later spreading out in the direction of the Huasteca and Pánuco. The Dominicans, who followed them, constructed monasteries throughout Oaxaca; that is, the Mixtec and Zapotec regions and the kingdom of Tututepec. The Augustinians, who reached Mexico when large parts of the territory were already occupied by the other two orders, had to be more dispersed. In central Mexico they were active with the Matlazinca and Otomí Indians as far as the sierra of Puebla and they occupied some of the areas of Michoacán not taken by the Franciscans. The stages and directions of the spiritual conquest can be traced by locating on the map the monasteries of the different orders. There are two great lines clearly indicating the Franciscan and Dominican advance to west and south, inter-mingled with monasteries of the Augustinians, whose task was to seal the evangelization of territories.

Each of the orders left a distinctive stamp on its areas. The Franciscan fortresses with their sixteenth-century plateresque facades and the sumptuous constructions of the Dominicans were built in population centers. Later, with the decimation of the Indians that began at the moment of their contact with the Spaniards and reached its climax at the beginning of the seven-teenth century, many of these centers were depopulated and the great monasteries have remained, as we see them today, forsaken in the countryside.

These missionaries left their imprint not only on the architec-ture of their monasteries but on many other aspects of the life of the region. During the sixteenth century they constructed hydraulic engineering works, large dams, and complex irrigation systems in central and western Mexico (Yuriria), some of which are still in use today; they also introduced the cultivation of certain types of vegetables and fruit trees. Because it fell to the missionary and the priest to direct the community activities and define the new forms of social organization of these conquered people, they soon became the hub of Indian life.

The sixteenth century, the century of conquest, was therefore the period when the social relations of the Indians were redesigned. The military conquest and the spiritual conquest, integral parts of the same process, laid down the general lines of action that would be followed in New Spain.

3

THE COLONIAL ECONOMY, 1650-1750

THE PRINCIPAL ECONOMIC structures of New Spain were established in the seventeenth century. During that period the hacienda was consolidated as the principal production unit after a long process of successive adaptations to the conditions of the colonial economy. In New Spain, as in other American colonies, there was a very small market for agricultural products. The Spanish and mestizo inhabitants of the cities, mine workers, and draft animals were practically the only consumers of the grain cereals produced by the hacienda. The Indians, who were the majority of the population, were not part of this market because they continued to consume the corn that they grew on their communal lands.

In addition to these market limitations, Mexico was a country without irrigated land, where crops depended largely on the frequency and abundance of rainfall. Much of the high plateau land was subject to such climatic phenomena as hail, frost, cloudbursts, floods, and droughts, which meant that bountiful years for agriculture were very irregular.

Therefore, the wealthy farmers of the colony chose the hacienda as the production unit that would enable them to cope with the limitations of the market and the uncertainties of seasonal crops. From the beginning, their determination to accumulate as much land as possible served a precise economic function: it controlled large extensions of land that could be used for various crops in addition to stands of trees for firewood and charcoal and fields for grazing and for raising maguey. Some owners had sufficient land to grow crops of both temperate and tropical climates, so that the income of the hacienda did not depend on a single crop. These secondary crops ensured the hacienda a small but stable income throughout the year and a larger profit margin in good harvest years.

Land accumulation by the hacienda had another economic consequence. As the hacienda increasingly took over large extensions of land, more and more people lost any possibility of having land of their own to farm. In this way, the hacienda not only monopolized production but, by despoiling the Indians of their land, it forced them into the cities and the consumption of urban products. Land accumulation also required a reliable supply of farm labor within a given hacienda.

One of the conditions underlying the entire colonial period, which explained the emergence of many institutions, was the decline in population. Although it has not been possible to measure the dimensions of the demographic crisis, we know that the population of New Spain did not return to its pre-Hispanic levels until the second half of the eighteenth century. Because the population was not only sparse but scattered in the rural areas, every possible means was used to keep labor on the hacienda land. The most effective method was to pay the agricultural worker such low wages that any special need, family celebration, or extra expense would compel the worker to ask for a loan from the hacienda owner. The latter knew he would never be repaid; but he also knew that by granting the loan he initiated an indebtedness that would bind the worker to the hacienda forever. This perpetual indebtedness was institutionalized through the *tienda de raya* ("company store").

The hacienda, furthermore, filled a number of societal functions that guaranteed the submission of the worker and the permanence of the institution. It offered the hired peon a security that he could not have on the land of his community. Whereas on the hacienda his family's subsistence was assured, as an independent worker left to his own resources he would be subject to the instability of the market and to agricultural cycles. With a bad harvest, he would have to abandon his land in order to survive and he would go to the city to swell the ranks of the urban disinherited and unemployed.

Thus, the hacienda took its form from the economic and social conditions of the colony. The development of other economic activities in the colony depended to a greater extent on the requirements of Spain. A good example of this was the *obraje* (factory).

From the beginning, the Spanish Crown prohibited the development of manufacturing in its American colonies as a means of protecting industrial development in Spain. Nevertheless, its manufactured goods, especially textiles, arrived in New Spain after a long voyage across the Atlantic and at prices so high that they could be purchased by only a privileged minority living in the major cities. Therefore, the colonies soon began to open *obrajes* that made coarse wool and cotton cloth for the use of the large population of poor people. In this sense, the royal prohibition served as a protectionist barrier and *obrajes* multiplied during the colonial period. The most important manufacturing centers were located in Mexico City and Puebla and in some places in the Bajío. Even though New Spain had begun to produce silk cloth in the sixteenth century, the cultivation and manufacture of silk in the colony was forbidden after contact was established with the Far East through the Manila galleon. In the seventeenth century the old silk looms of Puebla were converted into looms to produce the wool and cotton materials that were consumed in all the cities of the Viceroyalty.

Like the hacienda, the *obraje* was affected by a limited market and by the competition of the cloth woven by the Indians themselves; and the *obraje* owners similarly tried to prevent their workers from leaving. However, the exploitation of Indians in the *obraje* was far worse than on the hacienda. The owner recruited his labor among the delinquents sentenced to corporal punishment who served their sentences by working as prisoners in an *obraje*. This kind of labor was supplemented by the Negro slaves who were increasingly imported into New Spain.

Although limited, a market for the manufactured products of the *obraje* and for the cereal crops of the hacienda existed in the colony itself. The purpose of the other activity that supported the economy of New Spain, mining, was to meet the needs of the economy of the Spanish metropolis.

Mining played a basic role in the development of the colonial economy. Mining centers generated a great deal of agricultural activity. In northern Mexico, haciendas grew up around mines to supply the needs of the workers and draft animals; and the fortune of many haciendas was linked to that of the mines during much of the colonial period. Furthermore, taxes paid by mining activity were the main support of the administrative machinery of the colony and this revenue became more important with the expansion of the colonial bureaucracy in the seventeenth century.

The mining boom, which began with the discovery of Zacatecas in 1545 and reached its peak in the 1570s, ended early in the seventeenth century. From 1650 to 1750, mining in New Spain completely stagnated. During these years it could not compete with Peruvian silver output for several reasons. In the first place, New Spain did not have extensive deposits of quicksilver, which was needed to extract silver from ore by the patio process of amalgamation. In addition, importation of the quicksilver required by the mines of New Spain enormously increased production costs. In this same period, many of the old veins of silver that had been worked since the sixteenth century became exhausted or extremely deep. Because of the limited technical knowledge of the time, a very deep vein, which could be easily flooded, was not economical. The drop in mining productivity, combined with the population loss, explains the decline of the colonial economy in the second half of the seventeenth century.

The mines that remained in operation during this period were the same ones that had been exploited since the second half of the sixteenth century. The mines to the south of the volcanic mountain chain—Taxco, Sultepec, Temascaltepec, and Zacualpan—continued to produce silver, although in more difficult conditions. The mines in the north—Zacatecas, Fresnillo, Sombrerete, and Catorce—maintained their high productivity and gave rise to new mining towns like Durango and Chihuahua.

Life for the mine worker was very different from that of the agricultural worker on the hacienda or the urban worker in the *obraje*. The mine worker always kept his freedom of movement. Many were Indians who had abandoned their traditional villages and by living in mining centers were able to evade the head tax levied on the Indian population. High salaries were generally paid in mines, and through a system of *buscones* (searchers), workers could share in the exploitation of a vein, receiving payment in proportion to the amount of metal they extracted.

For these reasons, mining centers attracted large numbers of workers from distant regions who sought temporary or permanent jobs. Work in the mines, however, was uncertain and risky, and "bonanzas" led to a great deal of speculation and swindling.

Although mining generated activity within the colony, its product always went out of the country. Coins or ingots departed annually for Spain with the royal armada, leaving New Spain without specie. This situation directly affected trade.

During the colonial period, trade in New Spain was carried on according to a monopolistic and centralized scheme. Within the colony it reproduced the structure of Spain's trans-Atlantic trade, which began to operate toward the end of the sixteenth century. Under this system the Crown, which wanted as much revenue as possible from trade transactions, decreed that all merchandise going to the colonies should embark from a single port—Seville until the eighteenth century and later Cádiz. In this way, it could collect taxes on products that had not been manufactured in Spain. Sevillian merchants were often simply intermediaries for other European merchants and the Spanish port became a transit point for goods from England, France, and Holland, which thereby bypassed the prohibition on trade with the American colonies.

Within the colonial trade system designed by the Spanish Crown, products sent to the American market as well as the precious metal brought back to Spain had to travel in a fleet accompanied by numerous armed ships. This was to protect the cargo of gold and silver against capture by the English and Dutch pirates who might try to ambush the fleet on its return voyage. Maintaining a system of this kind was very costly and it had to be financed by raising the prices of products exported to the colonies, with the price going up as the distance increased. Furthermore, such an expensive system permitted only one voyage a year and so there was always a shortage of the European products needed by the colonies.

The trade of the colony with Spain was determined by a particular situation of limited supply and a captive market. Therefore, the metropolitan country could sell its European products at exorbitant prices with the certainty that they would be purchased in the colony. Once a year, with the arrival of the trans-Atlantic fleet or the trans-Pacific galleon, the cities of Jalapa and Acapulco took on the appearance of great trade fairs. Because only the powerful monopolistic merchants of the capital could buy the imported products in large lots and hold them for gradual sale during the rest of the year, Mexico City was the center of commercial activity throughout the colonial period.

Therefore, the seventeenth century—the century of "depression," the "unknown" and "forgotten" century—was precisely the period in which the principal structures of our colonial history were defined. It was then that the scheme of domination was consolidated and the mechanisms of a dependent economy were established.

Bibliography

ANNA, Timothy E. *The Fall of the Royal Government in Mexico City*. Lincoln, University of Nebraska Press, 1978.

BORAH, Woodrow. *New Spain's Century of Depression*. Norwood Editions, 1976.

BRADING, David A. *Miners and Merchants in Bourbon Mexico, 1763-1810*. Cambridge, England, The University Press, 1971.

——. *Haciendas and Ranchos in the Mexican Bajío: Leon, 1700-1860*. Cambridge, Cambridge University Press, 1978.

CHEVALIER, François. *Land and Society in Colonial Mexico: The Great Hacienda*. Translated by Lesley B. Simpson. Berkeley, University of California Press, 1963.

COOK, Sherburne F. and Woodrow BORAH. *Essays in Population History: Mexico and the Caribbean*. Vol. 2. Berkeley, University of California Press, 1974.

—— and Lesley Byrd SIMPSON. *The Population of Central Mexico in the Sixteenth Century*. New York, AMS Press, 1978.

COOPER, Donald. *Epidemic Disease in Mexico City, 1761-1813: An Administrative, Social, and Medical Study*. Austin, Texas, Institute of Latin American Studies, 1965.

CORTÉS, Hernando. *Fernando Cortés: His Five Letters of Relation to the Emperor Charles V (1519-1526)*. Translated and edited by Francis Augustus MacNutt. New Mexico, Rio Grande Press, 1977.

DÍAZ DEL CASTILLO, Bernal. *The Discovery and Conquest of Mexico, 1517-1521*. Translated by A. P. Maudslay. New York, Farrar, Straus and Giroux, 1979.

GIBSON, Charles. *The Aztecs under Spanish Rule. A History of the Indians of the Valley of Mexico, 1519-1810*. Stanford, California, Stanford University Press, 1976.

GREENLEAF, Richard E., ed. *The Roman Catholic Church in Colonial Latin America*. Tempe, Arizona State University Press, 1977.

HAMNETT, Brian R. *The Mexican Bureaucracy Before the Bourbon Reforms, 1700-1770: A Study in the Limitation of Absolutism*. Scotland, University of Glasgow Press, 1979.

HOWARD, David. *The Royal Indian Hospital of Mexico City*. Tempe, Arizona State University Press, 1980.

HUMBOLDT, Alexander. *Political Essay on the Kingdom of New Spain*. Lexington, University of Kentucky Press, 1957.

IRVING, Leonard A. *Baroque Times in Old Mexico: Seventeenth-Century Persons, Places, and Practices.* Westport, Connecticut, Greenwood Press, 1981.

KONRAD, Herman W. *A Jesuit Hacienda in Colonial Mexico: Santa Lucía, 1576-1767.* Stanford, California, Stanford University Press, 1980.

MACLACHLAN, Colin M. and Jaime E. RODRÍGUEZ O. *The Forging of the Cosmic Race: A Reinterpretation of Colonial Mexico.* Berkeley, University of California Press, 1981.

PRESCOTT, W. H. *The Conquest of Mexico.* London, J. M. Dent & Sons, 1978.

SHERMAN, William L. *Forced Native Labor in Sixteenth-Century Central America.* Lincoln, University of Nebraska Press,1979.

SIMPSON, Lesley Byrd. *Exploitation of Land in Central Mexico in the Sixteenth Century.* Berkeley, University of California Press, 1952.

———. *The Encomienda in New Spain: The Beginning of Spanish Mexico.* Berkeley, University of California Press, 1966.

SOLÍS, Antonio de. *The History of the Conquest of Mexico by the Spaniards.* New York, AMS Press, 1973.

TAYLOR, William B. *Drinking, Homicide, and Rebellion in Colonial Mexican Villages.* Stanford, California, Stanford University Press, 1979.

VAUGHAN, Thomas, E. A. P. CROWNHART-VAUGHAN and Mercedes PALAU DE IGLESIAS. *Voyages of Enlightenment: Malaspina on the Northwest Coast.* Portland, Oregon Historical Society, 1977.

III. THE PERIOD OF FORMATION

Luis González y González

1

THE CENTURY OF ENLIGHTENMENT

IN 1740, AFTER TWO HUNDRED years as a dependent part of the Spanish Empire, New Spain (or Mexico, as it is called today) entered an era of changes known as the Century of Enlightenment. In this century, which extended from the reign of Fernando VI (1746-1759) and the Viceroyalty of Francisco de Güemes, Count of Revillagigedo (1746-1755) to the reign of Carlos IV (1788-1808) and the Viceroyalty of José de Iturrigaray (1803-1808), New Spain increased its territory, population, and wealth; changed its political system; engendered a new social group; gained in wisdom and self-knowledge; and prepared itself for a separate and independent life from the Spanish nation.

The Mexicans of the eighteenth century wanted to emulate the conquests of the Spaniards of the sixteenth century. In 1721 they subdued the Indians of Nayarit and declared the vast province of Texas to be part of New Spain. A little later, José de Escandón conquered Nuevo Santander or Tamaulipas. Finally, in order not to be outdone by the Russians who came southward from Alaska and by the English who expanded from their colonies in northeastern North America, they organized expeditions to explore and study the coastal zones of the North Pacific and they promoted Jesuit and Franciscan missions in the huge California region. Although these eighteenth-century undertakings were not as spectacular as the conquests of the sixteenth century, they doubled the size of the territory of New Spain to more than one and a half million square miles, making it the largest of the Spanish-American countries and second only to Brazil in all the Americas.

Despite devastating epidemics such as the plague of 1735-1737 that caused a million deaths, in the Century of Enlightenment Mexico's population rose from two to six million inhabitants. This tripling of population was due less to territorial expansion than to increased immigration of Spaniards and to natural growth. From the beginning of the eighteenth century, significant groups of poor immigrants arrived from Spain—no longer from Andalusia and Extremadura as in the sixteenth and seventeenth centuries but from the northern provinces of Asturias, Galicia, and the Basque country. The new Creoles (*criollos*) of Basque, Asturian, and Galician descent made up a substantial group by the end of the eighteenth century. In 1800 Creoles amounted to one million or 16 percent of the total population and at least half of them lived in cities. The urban development of Mexico City was due to Creoles, who numbered more than 100,000; in Puebla they came to 70,000; in Guanajuato to 50,000; in each of the cities of Guadalajara, Zacatecas, Oaxaca, and Valladolid there were more than 20,000.

Indians continued to make up 60 percent of the population and mestizos 20 percent. The great century of *mestizaje* had been the sixteenth. In any event, the mestizos of the eighteenth century always outnumbered the Creoles and they also sought the shelter of cities. Negroes and mulattoes remained an ignominious minority living in the tropics and the mining towns.

New Spain grew and prospered in the Century of Enlightenment. In addition to territorial and population growth, the value of its economic output went up six times. Mining, still enslaving and inhuman, produced 3.300,000 pesos in 1670, 13.700,000 in 1750, and 27.000,000 in 1804. The silver production of Mexico equalled that of the rest of the world. Industry developed, especially in the field of textiles. The textile mills of Mexico City, Guadalajara, Querétaro, Oaxaca, and Valladolid expanded and progressed as did the manufacture of ceramics and wrought iron in Puebla, Guadalajara, and Oaxaca, together with the relatively novel production of *aguardiente* and tobacco.

An idea of the advance in foreign trade can be gathered from the following data: whereas in the 1740s only 222 ships docked at

Veracruz, in the 1790s that number rose to almost 1,500. A more liberal commercial policy beginning in 1765 encouraged foreign trade, which was all or almost all in the hands of *gachupines*, as the metropolitan Spaniards were derisively known in Mexico.

The Century of Enlightenment did not affect the agriculture of the Indian communities, where corn crops and maguey plantings neither increased nor improved. The agriculture of the Creoles, which was the wheat, sugar cane, and tobacco grown on the haciendas, progressed slowly by adding crops like coffee and some new farming techniques. Neither was the livestock industry, which continued as before, responsible for the prosperity displayed by Mexico in the final years of the Colony; its wealth could be seen in the last baroque and the first neoclassic constructions and above all in the increase in royal revenues, which went up from 5 500 000 pesos in 1763 to 20 000 000 in 1792. By 1800 Mexico had become one of the richest countries in the world, a country of "much wealth and maximum poverty."

The Spanish kings, especially Carlos III who ruled from 1759 to 1788, the viceroys of New Spain—especially the Marquises of Cruillas and Croix who governed successively from 1760 to 1771; Bucareli, viceroy in the 1770s; Matías de Gálvez, in the 1780s; and the second Count of Revillagigedo, from 1789 to 1794—all attributed the progress of the Colony to an enlightened despotism consisting of a dozen political-administrative practices. The sluggish Council of the Indies was replaced by the dynamic Ministry of the Office of the Indies. It not only sent active and energetic viceroys to New Spain but it established the *intendencia*, a regional body of authority and development. In 1786 the country was divided into *intendencias*, which were to be the basis of its future division into states. At the head of each division was placed an *intendente* charged with drawing up topographical maps of his province, making regional economic studies, distributing scientific and technical information to the public, building roads and other infrastructure works, beautifying cities, and punishing vagrants and wrongdoers.

Under the new policy, the first census of the Mexican population was taken in the latter part of the eighteenth century, economic reports and papers of every kind were written, maps were designed, scholarships and grants were awarded to researchers and students, information was gathered and circulated to combat disease and reform economic life, capital and technology were brought to mining, the Royal School of Mines was founded, mining engineers were imported from Germany, the explosives factory of Santa Fe was built as well as the School of Textiles in Tixtla, the Botanical Garden of Mexico, the School of Fine Arts, and other scientific, educational, and innovative institutions.

At another level, filth was not altogether eliminated, although the dreaded shout of "water on the way," which announced the dumping of urine or excrement from window to street, was heard less often. The city of Mexico, with more than 100 000 inhabitants, began to change in appearance and customs. It had many palatial residences, streets for coach traffic, and night illumination. The upper class began to copy the habits of the French. In the train of the Spanish governors came French cooks, hairdressers, and tailors. Because of French influence it became fashionable to have evening receptions and country picnics, retinues and martial displays. Not to be outdone by Paris, billiard and pool parlors appeared as well as places where one could go to play cards, or have a meal, a drink, or a coffee. Upper-class women, formerly so austere and withdrawn, who never left their homes except to call on a friend or attend church, began to gather for gossip, flirtations, and other frivolities. The women of the common people hardly changed, but their husbands began to drink heavily. Music was everywhere and dancing by couples began to replace the old dances and jigs. The Century of Enlightenment was famous for its public festivals and its huge private parties.

Nevertheless, the territorial expansion, economic prosperity, political-administrative reforms, and new customs benefitted only a fraction of the neo-Spanish population. In the Century of Enlightenment, Mexico grew and improved for a minority of fair-skinned people born in Spain and some of their descendants. Apart from these, the other Mexicans were worse off or remained the same—chained for life to the hacienda or community, mistreated in the *obraje*, enslaved in the mine and sugar mill, with no hope of freedom, fortune, or education.

In 1803, Alexander von Humboldt, a young German scholar visiting Mexico, found a large and wealthy country, leading the world in gold and silver production, but with most of its inhabitants poor and ignorant. When Humboldt left the supreme Spanish possession in America, he declared far and wide: "Mexico is a country of inequities; there is no equality in the distribution of wealth and culture."

The Bishop of Valladolid, who was a contemporary of Humboldt although less colorful and famous than the German scientist, said that in Mexico there were only two groups: "Those who have nothing and those who have everything." To the first group belonged the five million Indians, mestizos, and mulattoes, as well as about a million whites. To the second group of power and wealth belonged some 20,000 Spaniards who held the positions of authority and ran commerce and trade, together with about 10,000 Creoles who were owners of enormous haciendas and rich silver and gold mines. The Bishop did not include in his classification the tiny middle class, the only product of the Century of Enlightenment which would be of use to the Indians, mestizos, mulattoes, Negroes, and impoverished Creoles. This new human species would undertake in the eighteenth century a philanthropic task comparable to the charity of the sixteenth-century missionaries, not to please God but for humanitarian reasons.

First to profit from the changes of the century were the Spanish residents of New Spain who, as governors, increased their power or, as merchants, enhanced their wealth. Also benefitted were the Creole aristocrats who owned mines and haciendas. Finally, thanks to the culture of the Enlightenment, ordinary Creoles began to form the nucleus of a middle class and became the most dynamic part of the population. These new humanists began as a few clerics and grew to number thousands in the various religious orders and sectors of the lay society, including physicians, lawyers, merchants, and army officers.

Around 1760, the young Jesuits of New Spain became emotionally separated from Old Spain and transferred their respect and devotion to Mexico. They proclaimed themselves to be descendants of the Aztec Empire and fathers and brothers to the Indians, whom they treated as equals. The Creole Jesuit, Pedro José de

Márquez, maintained that "true philosophy does not recognize that any man has less ability because he was born white or black or because he was educated at the poles or in the tropics." Father Francisco Xavier Clavijero stated that Indians were "just as capable of learning all the sciences" as Europeans.

In addition to being pro-Indian, the budding patriotism of these men was telluric. They burst with love for the geography of Mexico. They believed that their country was a paradise, a fountain of eternal youth, a horn of plenty; in brief, "the best country under the sun." They cried out: "Mexican people, be content that your soil yields to no other. Think of how healthy it is, of its abundance of pure food and water, its mild climate, its beautiful contours." Even those like Father Juan Luis Maneiro, who acknowledged the underdevelopment of Mexico, said with pride: "I would trade Rome, famous world capital, for the wretched village of Tacuba."

A third feature of the Jesuits was their intellectual liberalism as opposed to the strait-jacketed ecclesiastic mentality. Father Rafael Campoy proposed that they "look for the truth, thoroughly investigate everything, unravel mysteries, distinguish between what is certain and what is questionable, scorn the inveterate prejudices of man, and advance from one field of knowledge to another." To carry out this ambitious program, his colleagues decided to read the European philosophers and scientists, from whom they learned study, research, and teaching methods.

In 1767, Carlos III decreed the expulsion of the Jesuits from all his domains. The Marquis de Croix, viceroy of New Spain, summoned the printer, Antonio de Hogal. He led the latter to a balcony of the Palace and delivered to him the originals of the edict, saying, "This is to be printed at once in your home in the knowledge that if you reveal its content before it is published tomorrow, I shall have you hung from this very balcony." The edict ordered the immediate departure of the Jesuits and its heading read: "Let it be known by the following that the subjects of His Majesty, King of Spain, were born to be silent and to obey in silence and not to discuss and express opinions on the high affairs of the government."

After the Jesuits were expelled, some of their former students—who in 1767 were twenty to forty years old, not all wealthy, and in the main not priests—carried on the reforms initiated by their teachers. At the forefront of a generation of Creole humanists dedicated to individual private study, modern experimental science, and objective journalism were men like Benito Díaz de Gamarra, author of the celebrated *Errores del entendimiento humano* (Errors of Human Understanding); the encyclopedist, José Antonio Alzate; the physician and mathematician, José Ignacio Bartolache; the astronomers, Antonio León y Gama and Joaquín Velázquez de Cárdenas; and the physicist, José Mariano Mociño. Thanks to this new group of Mexican scholars, enlightened institutes like the School of Mines and the Botanical Garden no longer echoed with "the wild outcries of someone who thought he had stumbled on the truth." Rhetoric and heavy tomes were also abandoned as a means of expression and propaganda. The new intellectuals had their work published in short-lived journals: *Mercurio Volante* (The Winged Mercury), *Asuntos varios sobre ciencias y artes útiles* (Various Matters Concerning the Sciences and Useful Arts), the famous *Gaceta de Literatura* (The Literary Gazette), and other media devoted to disseminating practical knowledge to modernize the economy of Mexico.

In 1786 the famine that every eleven years struck Indians, Negroes, and *castas* (mixed-breed) culminated in the "great famine." Crop failure due to scanty rainfall and severe frosts drove the majority of the population "to eat roots and grass like animals"; families disintegrated, many women were forced "to sell sons and daughters for two or three *reales*," and more than 100 000 Mexicans died. Hardly was the famine over than the government, seeing the French Revolution as the dangerous fruit of the Age of Enlightenment, decided to put a halt to reform and progress.

The suppression proved to be counterproductive. The young Creoles born between 1748 and 1764 refused to accept the return of tyranny, denounced the spectacle of the famine, and were attracted to the solutions offered by the French Revolution and by the independence of the thirteen British colonies in North America. The new Creole generation continued to study Mexico but, unlike its predecessors, it did so by using statistics to analyze the society and state of the country. It continued to be interested in Mexico's progress but also in its becoming an honorable nation.

The outcome of the political and social study was that Mexico was a country with a disgraceful present and a rosy future. Its present was social inequality, political despotism, and dependence on Spain. Mexico with its fabulous wealth would open up for itself a splendid future by removing despotism and inequality the French way and by eliminating dependence the North American way. To redress inequality, the Creole humanists proposed that tutelage of the Indians be ended and that all be made equal before the law, that communal lands be divided and given in private property to those who had shared its ownership, and that a system of *laissez faire* and *laissez passer* be followed. The doctrine of popular sovereignty was put forth against political despotism, and the advantages to be gained by separating from Old Spain were advanced in opposition to continued dependence.

The idea of independence spread and produced the first uprisings. In 1793 a conspiracy of two hundred Creoles was discovered in Guadalajara; it was headed by Father Juan Antonio de Montenegro, Vice-Rector of the local College of St. John the Baptist. In Mexico City there was the conspiracy of the accountant Juan Guerrero in 1794, followed five years later by the Machete Conspiracy, which was joined by many people for the purpose of waging a war that would get rid of the Europeans. Especially after 1796, hostility toward the Spanish regime grew steadily in the capital and in the major cities of the province. In that year, when Spain went to war with Great Britain and had to suspend export of its manufactured goods to Mexico, the Mexicans found that they were better supplied by ships from other countries and that their local industries could replace cheaply much of what had been imported. Independence began to seem less an ideal than a possibility. Nevertheless, the majority of Creoles awaited a more opportune moment to declare their nation's independence, because they did not want to pay too high a price. But what man proposed, circumstances disposed. What the Creoles wanted to have quickly and easily, they obtained only after years of difficult, bloody, and very destructive fighting.

THE REVOLUTION OF INDEPENDENCE

MIDDLE-CLASS CREOLES, as we have seen, were obsessed with the idea of independence. But even the rich Creole owners of haciendas and mines did not want to share the wealth of their country with the people of the Spanish nation. They all had a common goal: to give the orders in their own house and to be master of all its furnishings. The opportunity to free themselves from the yoke came in 1808, which was the year that Napoleon, one of the greatest conquistadors of all time, occupied Spain. The Spaniards fought the invader; and the Mexicans, who no longer felt themselves to be Spanish, tried to take advantage of this crisis to become independent, as may be seen in the verses that one morning appeared on the walls of the capital: "Open your eyes, Mexican people, and use this opportunity. Beloved compatriots, fate has placed freedom in your hands; if you do not shake off the Spanish yoke, you will be wretched indeed."

At about the same time, friar Melchor de Talamantes circulated subversive literature in which he declared that because Mexico had "all the resources and abilities needed to ensure the sustenance, preservation, and happiness of its inhabitants," it could become independent. He went on to say that independence was not only possible but desirable because the Spanish government was not as concerned with the general welfare of New Spain as would be a free government set up by the Mexicans themselves. To deal with this situation, the viceroy called a series of juntas of representatives of the colony. The *ayuntamiento* (town council, generally called *cabildo* in the colonies) proposed in these juntas that a national congress be convened. Having accepted but not acted on the idea, the viceroy was deposed on the night of September 15, by a wealthy Spanish merchant and *hacendado* and his following of peons, office workers, and *gachupines*. The Spaniard imprisoned the patriots Francisco Azcárate, Primo de Verdad, and Melchor de Talamantes and he took the liberty of appointing as successors to the viceroy first a high-ranking army officer and then the top cleric of the country.

The coup d'état was counterproductive. While Spaniards denounced Creoles before the internal security committee that had been appointed to judge and punish those suspected of disloyalty, middle-class Creoles decided to resort to revolutionary solutions.

Plots were widespread, but it was the conspirators of Querétaro, San Miguel, and Dolores who, when they were discovered, first took up arms. The morning of Sunday, September 16, 1810, the cleric and teacher Miguel Hidalgo y Costilla, an old man who was well-to-do, influential, and brilliant, had studied with the Jesuits, and was priest of the village of Dolores, freed the prisoners and locked up the Spanish authorities. Calling his parishioners to mass, he urged them from the portal of his church to join a "cause" dedicated to the overthrow of bad government. This exhortation is officially known as the "Grito de Dolores" and is considered the high point in Mexican history.

Hidalgo left his parish with 600 followers but within a few days they had swelled to about 100,000 men—both Creole and darker skinned—from mines, haciendas, and *obrajes*. Although this multitude seemed to be more a mass demonstration armed with shovels and slings than an army, it encountered no resistance in San Miguel, Celaya, and Salamanca. The important mining city, Guanajuato, fell after a bloody battle and was pillaged.

The Bishop of Michoacán excommunicated Hidalgo, but the latter led his "army" against the Michoacán capital and forced the cathedral council to lift his excommunication. After Valladolid, he set out for Mexico City, which was relatively unprotected. He won the battle of Monte de las Cruces, requested a parley with the viceroy and then, without waiting for a reply, ordered a retreat during which he was defeated in San Jerónimo Aculco by the Spanish General Félix María Calleja.

Meanwhile, there had been uprisings in many parts of the country. Rafael Iriarte led insurgents in León and Zacatecas, and the friars Herrera and Villerías took possession of San Luis Potosí. In the northwest Juan B. Casas arrested the governor of Texas, in Nuevo León the governor declared its independence, and viceregal troops defected in Coahuila and Tamaulipas. In central Mexico were the troops of Tomás Ortiz, Benedicto López, Julián and Chito Villagrán, Miguel Sánchez, and others. In the south José María Morelos, parish priest of Carácuaro and Nocupétaro, began his campaign. In the west there were three important movements. One was headed by José María Mercado, parish priest of Ahualulco, who captured Tepic and the port of San Blas. Another, under José María González Hermosillo, won almost all of Sinaloa, including the port of Mazatlán. The third was led by José Antonio Torres, born in the Bajío of Guanajuato, who entered Zamora with his army of insurgents. "The flower of Guadalajara youth" tried to stop them just outside of Zacualco. With their slings the Torres troops hurled such a shower of stones on the young men of Guadalajara that they killed many and put the rest to flight. Torres and his men entered Guadalajara on November 11, 1810.

After his defeat at Aculco, Hidalgo retired to Guadalajara where he issued decrees to give exclusive use of communal lands to their owners, to emancipate 6,000 Negro slaves, to eliminate state monopolies of tobacco, gunpowder, and playing cards, and to abolish the tributes paid by Indians. He also tried to organize a government, an army, and a newspaper. The army, composed of more than 30 000 men, was routed by Calleja's forces at Puente de Calderón. The remnants of the insurgent troops then set off for Zacatecas in search of support from Iriarte but, pursued by Calleja, they continued north where they fell into a trap that had been laid for them by the former chief of the independence movement of Coahuila. The captives were taken before a council of war and Hidalgo was condemned to death and executed on July 30, 1811.

Nevertheless, the fight for independence was carried on by Ignacio López Rayón, who tried to unite the insurgents in the Junta of Zitácuaro, and by a group who went to represent Mexico at a convention in Spain. While part of the Mexican population fought against the viceregal government with sticks and stones and whatever else they could lay their hands on, another part accepted the invitation of the new Spanish government that had emerged from the struggle against Napoleon to send delegates to a convention that was to meet in Cádiz in 1811. The sixteen representatives were all Creoles except one and they were mainly clerics and young men of the middle class. In Cádiz they demanded equality before the law for Spaniards and Spanish-Americans, the elimination of caste distinctions, equal justice for all, the construction of roads, industrialization, government of Mexico for the Mexicans, schools, the return of the Jesuits, a free press, and the declaration that "sovereignty resides in the people." Some of the Creole demands were accepted and incorporated into the constitution drafted by this convention in March 1812.

The Political Constitution of the Spanish Monarchy produced in Cádiz made Spain a constitutional monarchy. It gave real power to the executive branch and it took away the other two powers from the king. It was a liberal constitution guaranteeing individual rights, freedom of speech, and equal treatment for Spaniards and Spanish-Americans. Viceroy Venegas promulgated it in Mexico in September 1813 and immediately proceeded to hold elections for the *ayuntamientos*, the deputies to the Cortes, and the deputies to the five provincial districts that operated in Mexico. However, the Cádiz Constitution was too little and too late; and it remained in force for only about a year. Opposed by the Spanish group and by the wealthy Creoles, it was finally abolished in August 1814 by Viceroy Calleja, who succeeded Venegas. The reaction to this measure was to swell the ranks of the insurgents. On reestablishment of the authoritarian regime, several Creole intellectuals decided to join the army of the village priest Morelos. An intelligent but unlettered man who had been initially ignored and scorned, Morelos had been growing "in power and importance and, like those storm clouds born in the south, he soon covered a vast stretch of land." With the passionate support of his devoted followers, he waged brilliant campaigns in 1812 and 1813. In a lightning maneuver, he captured Oaxaca and seized General

González Saravia, supreme commander of the viceregal armies. On April 12, 1813, Acapulco fell to Morelos, who confirmed his victory with these words: "The nation wants to be governed by the Creoles and since it has not been heeded, it has taken arms to make itself understood and obeyed."

Everything seemed to indicate that the end of Spanish domination was imminent. Therefore, Morelos decided to convene a national assembly to give a political constitution to the nascent country. The Anáhuac Congress met for four months in Chilpancingo and it included such distinguished Creoles—both scholars and clerics—as Carlos María de Bustamante, former editor of the *Diario de México*; Ignacio López Rayón, former president of the Junta of Zitácuaro and author of *Elementos constitucionales* (Constitutional Elements); Father José María Cos, "a man of great talent and inventive genius," former editor of two insurgent newspapers; Andrés Quintana Roo, famous poet, journalist, and jurist; Sixto Verduzco, physician; José María Liceaga, army officer; and Father Manuel Herrera. At the opening of the convention, Morelos asked the delegates to declare that Mexico was free and independent of Spain, that Catholicism was the only true religion, that sovereignty was vested in the people, and that laws "should moderate opulence and poverty" and banish "ignorance, plunder, and theft." On November 6, the convention approved the Act of Independence and proclaimed that "there is not nor can there be peace with the tyrants."

Although Morelos left Chilpancingo the following day in search of new triumphs, his political activities had permitted Calleja to regroup and mobilize the troops of the viceroyalty. Morelos was defeated in Valladolid and the royalists advanced on the south. After wandering from place to place, the Congress reached Apatzingán in October, 1814, and announced the constitution, which had been inspired in the French constitution of 1793 and the Spanish constitution of 1812. In its first forty-one articles it declared Catholicism to be the state religion, the sovereignty of the people to be exercised through Congress, law to be the expression of general will, and the happiness of citizens to consist in enjoying equality, security, property, and liberty. Almost two hundred articles referred to the form of government, which was to be centralist republican and divided into three branches of power. The legislative, composed of seventeen deputies, was above the executive with three sharing the title of president, and the judicial commanded by a supreme court of five people.

The Apatzingán Constitution was never put into practice because by the time it was promulgated, the insurgents had been dislodged from the southern provinces and Morelos had only 1,000 men left to face Calleja's troops of 80,000. After a last desperate stand he was taken prisoner and executed on December 22, 1815, in San Cristóbal Ecatepec, near Mexico City.

With the death of the "Southern Thunderbolt," the struggle for independence lost the last of its famous leaders but not its fighting spirit. Groups continued the battle from fortified points and redoubts; others waged guerrilla warfare; and others made sudden and brilliant raids on the enemy. Father Marcos Castellanos reinforced his position on an island in Lake Chapala; Ramón Rayón dug in at Cóporo, where he fought off several attacks; Ignacio López Rayón was entrenched at Zacatlán; Manuel Mier y Terán retreated to Cerro Colorado, Pedro Moreno to Sombrerete, and Pedro Ascensio to Barrabás.

Outside the fortified strongholds, bands of Indians, mestizos, and mulattoes roamed the countryside. Driven by poverty and a desire for vengeance, they took over properties and murdered property owners. The troops of Villagrán and Osorno overran the outskirts of Pachuca and the plains of Apan. The followers of Gómez de Lara ("The Crate"), Gómez ("The Castrator"), Bocardo ("Colonel of the Colonels"), Arroyo, the Ortiz brothers, Olarte, Pedro el Negro, and others became notorious for their crimes. Detested by the rich Creoles, they nonetheless enjoyed the sympathy of most of the population. Francisco Xavier Mina, who came to New Spain in 1817 to fight "for liberty and for the interests of the Spanish Empire," went over to the insurgent side, taking with him the men, arms, and money he had brought from England and the United States. After winning battles as far as Guanajuato, he was taken prisoner and executed at Fuerte de los Remedios. Most of the leaders entrenched on islands, hilltops, and bluffs, were quickly disposed of. Castellanos surrendered at the end of 1816, and Rayón and Mier y Terán at the beginning of 1817. The forts at

Los Remedios and Jaujilla fell in 1818. Furthermore, Viceroy Apodaca, who succeeded Calleja, offered amnesty to resistance fighters, many of whom gave up their arms. Others, like Guadalupe Victoria, went into hiding and several were routed. By 1819 only a few minor guerrilleros like Pedro Ascencio and Vicente Guerrero continued to fight in the wilderness of the south.

Most of the Creoles had accepted defeat, when a new series of events put them on the road to independence, if not to liberty and social reform. In 1820, a liberal revolution forced Fernando VII to reestablish the Constitution of Cádiz. The Cortes, which was made up of fervent liberals, insisted on measures against the wealth and immunities enjoyed by the Church. News of these reforms caused consternation among the Spanish group and the Creole aristocracy of Mexico. Viceroy Apodaca refused to apply the Constitution of Cádiz and instead approved the Plan de La Profesa which declared that as long as the king was under pressure from revolutionaries, his viceroy in Mexico would govern with the Laws of the Indies and with complete independence from Spain. However, when Governor Dávila was forced to proclaim constitutional order in Veracruz, the viceroy declared the constitution to be in effect throughout the viceregal domain. He immediately proceeded to hold municipal elections and institute freedom of the press; and he thereby unwittingly set into motion the activity of organized groups. Spaniards who had supported the Plan de La Profesa tried to have it implemented, while rich Creoles saw the opportunity to achieve independence without the need to introduce social reforms. Both groups agreed that the leader to carry out their objectives was the Creole Colonel Agustín de Iturbide, a courageous, cruel, dissolute, and charming man who was never happier than when waging war.

Supported by the high clergy, the Spaniards, and the Creole owners of mines and haciendas, Iturbide, who had been commissioned to crush Guerrero, made a deal with the latter to join forces and together they announced the Plan of Iguala or the Three Guarantees: Roman Catholicism as the only recognized religion; equality of all Mexican citizens; and an independent Mexico with a constitutional monarch who would be a prefabricated king from one of the ruling houses of Europe. Then he launched a campaign on two fronts—diplomatic and military—which in five months had solved everything. The diplomatic consisted in gaining the friendship of the insurgent leaders against whom he had fought years earlier. The military campaign was brief and almost bloodless; many garrisons joined him willingly. Blaming Apodaca for the successes of Iturbide, the Spaniards in the capital again removed their viceroy, as in 1808, and they named Marshall Novella to replace him. A few days later, Juan O'Donojú arrived from Spain to take over the post of viceroy and he speedily came to terms with Iturbide. On August 24, 1821, he signed the Treaty of Córdoba, which ratified the substance of the Plan of Iguala. Iturbide led his victorious *trigarante* army into Mexico City on September 27, and the following day he was appointed head of the first independent government.

The consummation of independence produced great enthusiasm. In all the villages, towns, and cities there were parades with allegorical floats, triumphal arches, firework displays, and general rejoicing. Poets composed odes, sonnets, songs, marches, and verses in honor of the liberated nation. Several newspapers appeared and pamphlets were published; leaflets and letters obsessed with the subject of independence were circulated; there was talk of the wealth and economic resources of Mexico; it was said that the "location, fortune, and fertility of the new nation indicated that it had been created to give law to the whole world"; and it was announced that "the richest empire in the world was reestablished."

Iturbide was acclaimed as a "man of God," a "saintly man," and "father of the nation." Middle-class intellectuals wrote drafts of a political constitution and good laws; they drew up plans to promote agriculture, livestock raising, fishing, mining, trade, and public revenues; schemes to improve working conditions, to increase the population, and to extend education and health. Most of the projects took their inspiration from the experience of other nations. Some wanted to return to forms of Greek and Roman life, others believed that the model to follow was the young republic of the United States, several proposed that the Aztec Empire be emulated. Almost no one based his project on current Mexican realities. Perhaps none of the planners was aware at that time of the scarcity of natural resources, the lack of population, and above all the economic decline, social disruption, and political dislocation generated in the long struggle for independence. With very few exceptions, all closed their eyes to the obstacles and opened them only to see the advantages of independent life.

3

THE SANTA ANNA INTERLUDE

AT THE TIME it won its independence, Mexico was the largest of the Spanish-American countries; and in 1822, it added more than 180,000 square miles by incorporating the Central American provinces. Therefore, its geopolitical problems were enormous: international isolation; border difficulties; regional separatism; and deterioration of its roads. The Independence Wars had paralyzed its maritime traffic with the Far East, South America, and Europe. The Adams-Onís Treaty of 1819 did not precisely define its border with the United States, nor were the boundaries to the south clearly marked, especially its frontier with the English colony of Belize. Population did not grow during the Independence Wars, and in 1822 a territory of 1.730,000 square miles contained 7 million people. The war against Spain had cost 600,000 lives, which was a tenth of the total, or half the labor force. Population was not only sparse but, as in the colonial period, it was concentrated in central Mexico. No one wanted to go to the vast uninhabited northern region which presented an open invitation to plunder.

In the economic sphere, things were worse. Eleven years of war had reduced mining production from 30 million pesos in 1810 to 6 million. The value of agricultural output had been cut to one half and of industrial production to one third. In 1822 government revenues were 9.500,000 pesos and expenditures were 13.500,000. And as if an annual deficit of 4 million pesos were not enough, the emerging country inherited a public debt of 76 million. The drop in state revenues was not temporary; it was due largely to the abolition of an injustice, the head tax on Indians. Nor could the rise in state expenditures be temporary; it was now necessary to support a large and strong army to safeguard the nation's independence. The treasury was condemned to a state of chronic bankruptcy and to fall into the hands of usurers.

There were many problems to solve in the social sphere. The declaration of equal treatment for all Mexicans left the Indian, accustomed to a system of guardianship, at the mercy of the Creole. Equality of rights intensified inequality of fortunes. The 3,749 latifundia grew at the expense of the land of the Indian communities. Also, as was to be expected, laws of equality alone did nothing to improve the working conditions of the peon and the factory worker. On the other hand, civil strife had brought about a mixing of the races and a consolidation of the middle class. After 1821, it was the middle class that contested the power of the landed aristocracy.

Immediately following independence, political difficulties rose to the surface: the inexperience of Creoles in public administration; the tendency of minor caudillos to convert themselves into overlords of the regions where they had fought; the desire of the major caudillos to be king or president of the new country; the war between parties due to a complete lack of understanding between monarchists and republicans, the military and civilians, clerics and bureaucrats; the political indifference of most of the population; and the political extremism of the minority, especially the middle class.

The Government Junta, installed on September 28, 1821, and composed of 38 aristocrats, was authorized to elect members of the Regency, to set down the rules for convening and electing a Congress charged with drafting a political constitution, and to decide on the national insignia. It began with the flag, declaring its colors to be green, white and red, and it ended by convening a Congress, in which the majority of the deputies were middle-class Creoles imbued with French and North American revolutionary ideas and in favor of a republican form of government. The few monarchist deputies were divided between supporters of the Bourbon family and supporters of Iturbide. Congress inaugurated its sessions on February 24, 1822. When it shortly became known that the Spanish Cortes had refused to ratify the Treaty of Córdoba, considering it "illegitimate and void," the Bourbon adherents either withdrew from the political contest or transferred their support to Iturbide.

From then on events moved swiftly. Despite its majority of anti-monarchists, the Constitutional Congress elected Iturbide emperor with the title Agustín I and the latter, after a lavish coronation in May 1822, governed for eleven months. In August he learned of a plot against him involving some deputies; in October he dissolved Congress and named in its place a junta charged with preparing a provisional political code and with calling for the election of a new congress; in December one of his old cronies, Brigadier-General Antonio López de Santa Anna, rose up against him in Veracruz and declared for a republic; in January 1823 General Antonio Echávarri, sent by the emperor to combat Santa Anna, made a pact with the enemy; in March Agustín I doffed his crown, recalled the congress he had dismissed, and left the country; in April the deputies abolished the supreme executive power; in July the Central American provinces declared their independence; and in November 1823 a second congress proclaimed the Republic and drew up a constitution.

The Constitution of 1824 divided Mexico into nineteen states and five territories, with each state electing its own governor and legislative assembly as occurred in the United States and as had been provided for in the Constitution of Cádiz. The federal government exercised the three classic powers according to the doctrine of Montesquieu: the legislative power would be composed of a chamber of deputies and a senate; the executive would be held by a president or, in his absence, a vice-president; and the highest level of the judiciary would be the supreme court. As for principles, the Constitution of 1824 kept Catholicism as the state religion, prohibiting the practice of any other religion, and it decreed freedom of press and speech. Besides issuing an order to execute Iturbide—subsequently carried out by a handful of soldiers—it held the first elections, which chose as president and vice-president Guadalupe Victoria and Nicolás Bravo, two stalwart and worthy caudillos of the Independence Wars with no political experience.

During the administration of Guadalupe Victoria, Mexican independence was recognized by the United States and England, a panamerican union was proposed, the Spaniards were banished, and the Scottish Rite and York Rite masonic lodges engaged in a power struggle. The first three countries to send diplomatic representatives to Mexico were Chile, Colombia, and Peru. The fourth was the United States, represented by minister Joel R. Poinsett, who would become notorious for his interference in the internal politics of Mexico. A day before Poinsett, Henry Ward had presented his credentials as chargé d'affaires of England, and he too would dedicate himself to intrigue. The former worked to bring about sale of the northern Mexican provinces to the United States, the latter to obtain a more favorable commercial treaty for Great Britain. Poinsett, forerunner of the Monroe Doctrine, opposed any form of European intervention in the internal affairs of Mexico, but he also opposed the ideal of Bolívar to create a defensive and offensive alliance of the peoples of the Americas against aggressions by the Old World empires.

Although the fort of San Juan de Ulúa, Spain's last bastion in Mexico, had fallen to Mexican troops in 1825, neither Spain nor the Spaniards lost hope of reconquering the former colony. While Spain prepared military expeditions in Cuba, Spanish residents in Mexico conspired with their mother country. For this reason, the Mexican government decided to expel them and with their departure the economy lost the capital they had accumulated. In its place came heavy foreign indebtedness, British loans and machinery to revive the mining industry, and businessmen from Hamburg, France, England, and the United States.

At this time, the ruling classes of Mexico were concerned only with political matters and barely or not at all interested in economic and cultural affairs. The wealthy people who had supported Iturbide and the Bourbon monarchy—that is, the upper-class Creoles—founded masonic lodges of the Scottish Rite, which were centers for a political party with centralist tendencies. Drawing on the middle class, who far outnumbered the aristocracy, Poinsett established lodges of the York Rite to serve as the base for a federalist party. The battle between members of the two masonic orders continued throughout the four-year period of Victoria's administration, culminating in a revolt that demanded an end to the secret societies, the departure of Poinsett, and adherence to the constitution. This military uprising was led by Nicolás Bravo, vice-president of the Republic and head of the Scottish Order; and it was suppressed by General Vicente Guerrero, head of the York Masons. Once the leaders of the Scottish Masons had gone into exile, the York Masons took control of the situation and put forth the candidacies of both Manuel Gómez Pedraza and Vicente Guerrero for the presidency beginning in 1829. Gómez Pedraza won the election; but Vicente Guerrero, the man who "owed nothing to art and everything to nature," assumed the presidency by force, through a popular riot known as the "Acordada Mutiny." That same year he was faced with the problem of dislodging from Tampico a small expeditionary force of 4,000 men sent from Spain by Ferdinand VII to reconquer Mexico. After a savage battle, the Spaniards surrendered to General Santa Anna. Meanwhile, General Anastasio Bustamante, who commanded the reserve army against the invader, used his troops to overthrow Guerrero.

General Bustamante, another "complete incompetent," took office on the first day of 1830. He formed a strong government with the help of the young aristocrat Lucas Alamán, who proposed that the army be disciplined, public finance be reorganized, and a reconciliation be arranged with Spain and the Vatican in order to secure their recognition of Mexico's independence. Civil war broke out again. Former President Guerrero rebelled and fell into the hands of his enemies, who executed him, thereby prompting Santa Anna to lead a revolt in Veracruz. Bustamante was exiled and Gómez Pedraza, who replaced him and completed the term to which he had been elected four years earlier, held elections. Generals Mier y Terán and Santa Anna were both candidates, but the former committed suicide leaving the presidency to Santa Anna, the paranoid, romantic, restless *Yorkino* leader, the general who always "pronounced" for rebellions.

Santa Anna presided but he did not govern. Retiring to his hacienda in the countryside, he turned his power over to Vice-President Valentín Gómez Farías of the radical wing of the Creoles who, with the aid of such advisors as José María Mora, immediately launched a triple reform of Church, school, and army. Because it was considered that the clergy were too concentrated in cities to attend to the needs of the faithful in towns and villages, that the wealth of the Church amounting to 180 million pesos was not used for the common good, and that the clergy not only imposed burdensome contributions but limited freedom, it was decided to subordinate the Church to the government through a *Patronato*, to attach Church properties, and to eliminate the tithe. Because it was estimated that the Republic spent one million more than its total budget of 13 million pesos to maintain 5,000 soldiers and 18,000 officers who tyrannized the nation, the privileges of the army were abolished and regular troops were replaced by volunteers. Because it was believed that the educational monopoly of the religious orders was undesirable, they were no longer granted the exclusive right to teach.

Various pronouncements frustrated the reformist program of Mora and Gómez Farías. President Santa Anna himself, now as defender of those he had previously fought, marched against the vice-president, dismissed him, and suspended his laws. He soon had to face a major problem. In 1821 Moses Austin had been given permission to settle part of Texas with 300 non-Mexican families. This group expanded so rapidly that in twelve years they far outnumbered the Mexican residents in Texas. Most of these settlers came from the United States, were Protestant, spoke English, and hoped to live free of Mexican taxes and jurisdiction. When the Bustamante regime installed customs and small fortified garrisons, Stephen Austin, son of Moses, led a protest against the customs regulations; and the United States chargé d'affaires in Mexico asked for removal of the garrisons. In 1833 Austin persuaded the Mexican government to consider Texas a state separate from Coahuila and in 1835 he attacked and overcame the few Mexican troops quartered in the forts. Then President Santa Anna in person, with an army of 6,000 men, went forth to conquer the rebels. On several occasions he was successful in driving back the Texans and at the Alamo he needlessly massacred all its defenders. However, after his army was taken by surprise and destroyed at San Jacinto in 1836, he was compelled to sign the Velasco Treaties under which he agreed to suspend the war.

At the close of 1836, Congress replaced the Constitution of 1824 with the Seven Laws, which did away with state entities, strengthened presidential power, and restricted civil rights. In 1837 Bustamante was elected president in the midst of a turmoil of liberal pronouncements, Indian rebellions, and foreign claims and interventions. In 1838 a French naval force captured Veracruz in order to collect a bill owed to a pastry cook by the Bustamante government. In the so-called "Pastry War," General Santa Anna lost his left foot and, barely recovered from his wound, joined with other generals to overthrow Bustamante. After a brief rule, he turned the government over to Nicolás Bravo, reclaimed it, was expelled by one pronouncement and restored to power by another. Internal strife became chronic. Yucatán sought its independence from Mexico. A provisional executive (1841-1843) convened Congress, which in 1843 drafted a new constitution known as The Organic Laws, which remained in force for no more than three years.

Texas kept the independence it had won in 1836 until 1845, when the United States Congress admitted Texas into the Union over the opposition of the anti-slave states. Although the Mexican government had declared in 1843 that admission would be cause for war, the Mexican president in 1845 behaved as a model of prudence; but neither the Texans nor the Mexican public supported him. The former wanted to extend their territory beyond the Río Nueces, the recognized frontier, to the Río Grande. The Mexican generals believed that war was necessary and one of this group, General Paredes, became president in 1846, when the United States army crossed the Río Grande. Several thousand North Americans occupied Santa Fe in New Mexico; others, supported by a fleet in the Pacific, entered California; Los Angeles defended itself heroically but in vain. In the capital, Mexican generals fought over the presidency while one column of the invading army conquered the almost deserted provinces of New California, New Mexico, and Chihuahua. Another column, commanded by General Zachary Taylor, entered the country from the northeast and routed the Mexican Generals Arista, Ampudia, and Santa Anna.

The domestic crisis deepened. After funds for resistance were exhausted, Gómez Farías tried to raise money by taking over and mortgaging Church property. He was overthrown by a mutiny of the regiment of *polkos* (sons of devout, well-to-do families) and his expropriation decree was abrogated shortly after General Winfield Scott, at the head of a small expeditionary force, disembarked in Veracruz. Advancing slowly, the North Americans defeated Santa Anna at Cerro Gordo; successively occupied Perote, Jalapa, and Puebla; and in August reached the mountain plateau of Mexico City. Here they won a series of encounters at Padierna, Churubusco, and Chapultepec. This final battle was fought courageously by the cadets of the military college at Chapultepec Castle, who are still commemorated as the "Niños Héroes". On September 14, 1847, the flag of the United States was raised over the National Palace of Mexico City, while the vanquished government established itself in Querétaro.

On February 2, 1848, Mexico signed the Treaty of Guadalupe under which it surrendered to the United States an area of 890 000 square miles comprising Texas, New Mexico, and California, or more than half of its national territory. The United States gave Mexico 15 million dollars as compensation for this enormous territorial loss. There was deep pessimism in the conquered nation to the point of believing that it was incapable of governing itself or of defending itself from outside attacks. Lucas Alamán even declared: "We are lost beyond recall if Europe does not soon come to our aid." In thirty years of independence Mexico had enjoyed neither peace, nor economic development, nor social harmony, nor political stability.

From 1821 to 1850 Mexico was in a state of constant turmoil. In thirty years there were fifty governments, almost all the result of military coups and eleven of them presided over by General Santa Anna. The life of the country was at the mercy of feuding masonic lodges, ambitious army officers, audacious bandits, and raiding Indians. Generals produced battles wholesale to overthrow presidents and governors. Troops were recruited through "levies," in which peasants were rounded up and the youngest and strongest dispatched to the slaughter. Those who managed to desert generally became bandits until there were hundreds of marauding parties, mainly in the central region. In the peripheral zones, the scourge was the Indian; in the north, the Comanche, Apache, Yaqui, and

Mayo tribes. At the other end of the country, on the Yucatán peninsula where they had been savagely exploited by whites, the Maya Indians rose up in 1848 against their oppressors. The "War of Castes" lasted three years during which both sides robbed, killed, and pillaged without quarter.

In the midst of civil war, the economy of the country could not develop. Mining recovered thanks to British investments, the use of steam-driven machinery, and new smelting techniques. In industry, only a few factories of cotton textiles progressed. The Banco de Avío, founded by Alamán to encourage economic activity, was not successful. Communications and transport continued to deteriorate from 1821 until after 1850. Every region in Mexico produced strictly what was necessary to meet its requirements. Poverty and isolation were the norm in all sectors of human activity. Nonetheless, contacts with the outside world were greater than during the colonial period. Mexico's troubled waters were fished by tailors, merchants, shoemakers, and pharmacists from France, by tradesmen from Germany, and by businessmen from England.

Although public education abounded with good intentions, it showed few advances, and these were due mainly to the work of the Lancasterian Society; whereas the institutes of secondary and higher education in Oaxaca and Toluca were excellent, the older universities on Mexico and Guadalajara had declined. In literature, the most distinguished novelist was Joaquín Fernández de Lizardi; the best playwright was Manuel Eduardo Gorostiza; and the most famous poets were Quintana Roo, Pesado, and Carpio of the neo-classical school, as well as the romanticists Calderón and Rodríguez Galván. The field of history boasted four outstanding scholars: Alamán, Bustamante, Mora, and Zavala. Journalism attracted many aspiring writers and the most widely circulated newspapers were *El Sol*, *El Águila Mexicana*, *El Tiempo*, and *El Universal*. The Academy of San Carlos was reorganized in 1843 under the direction of the Catalonian, Clavé, and it was responsible for the formation of the artist Joaquín Cordero.

After three decades of independence, Mexico—dismembered, without peace or national unity—could pride itself only on its intellectuals. In the midst of the tumult, these "thinking people" kept their integrity and remained capable of daring and sacrifice.

4

THE REFORM

AROUND 1850 Mexican intellectuals became so alarmed by the loss of half of the country's territory, the poverty of its people and government, the disarray of its public administration, and its state of perpetual civil war that they decided to take into their hands the destiny of the sick nation.

There could not be many cultivated men in a society in which only one in ten knew how to read and write; and these few were theoreticians, not technicians. Most of them were priests, lawyers, or army men by profession and poets, orators, and journalists by vocation.

The educated class, although united in its desire to solve the serious national problems, was deeply divided when it undertook the task. As few as they were, the intellectuals formed two parties: Liberals and Conservatives. The Liberals were long-haired young lawyers with modest incomes, whereas most of the Conservatives were prosperous members of the Church or army, middle-aged and older, and regularly groomed at the barbershop. Both Conservatives and Liberals believed in the natural grandeur of their country and in the hopeless inadequacies of their countrymen. They agreed that Mexican society was not vigorous enough to save itself but their pessimism differed in kind and their programs of action were diametrically opposed.

The man adopted by the Conservative Party as its leader was the brilliant but ageing Lucas Alamán, who was exceptionally well qualified for the role. He had studied in Europe and was noted as a man of letters. He was dapper, solemn, and very devout. According to Arturo Arnaiz y Freg, because of his ability "to penetrate to the soul of people ... even his opponents respected him ... He could adapt himself with delicate flexibility to circumstances," and at the same time he lived "with anguished concern over the internal weakness of Mexico." He was supported by the more numerous if not the more enthusiastic part of the intellectuals. Lucas Alamán was the leader of cassocks and epaulets.

The Conservatives, perhaps because they had much to lose, did not want to risk breaking new trails for the country. They longed to return to the Spanish order and to live in the shadow of the Old World monarchies. Because they were traditionalists who wished to turn back to the European model, their enemies called them crabs and traitors. Alamán summed up their program in seven points: 1) We want "to preserve the Catholic religion ... to support its cult in splendor ... to ban by public authority the circulation of impious and immoral works"; 2) "We want the government to be sufficiently strong ... although subject to principles and responsibilities that prevent abuse"; 3) "We are opposed to the federal system, to the system of elected representatives ... and to everything that can be called popular election ..."; 4) "We believe in the necessity of a new territorial division that would eliminate present state boundaries and facilitate good administration"; 5) "We believe in a large enough army for the country's needs"; 6) "We want no more congresses ... only some planning advisors"; and 7) "We are lost beyond recall if Europe does not soon come to our aid."

Although in mid-century the Liberals did not have a leader, their Party already included some distinguished middle-aged members. One of these was Benito Juárez, born on March 21, 1806, of humble rural origins. He had been educated in a religious seminary and in the Institute of Arts and Science of Oaxaca; he had served as deputy to the Oaxacan Congress from 1832 to 1834, and to the Federal Congress ten years later. Still under forty were a number of other outstanding figures: the eminent philosopher and naturalist, Melchor Ocampo, born in 1814, a graduate of the religious seminary of Morelia, a man of property, lucid, intransigent, witty, and governor of Michoacán from 1846 to 1853; the dynamic and tough-minded Miguel Lerdo de Tejada, born in Veracruz in 1812, a student of history and economics, author of several books, president of the Lancasterian Society, and Minister of Development; and General Ignacio Comonfort, of the same age as Lerdo but, unlike the latter, given to moderation and compromise with no trace of Jacobinism, and scrupulously honest.

Differing from the Conservatives, the Liberals denied Spanish, Indian, and Catholic traditions; they believed in the existence of an irreconcilable antagonism between the historical antecedents of Mexico and its future greatness and in the need to lead the country along completely new paths of freedom of work, trade, education, and writing, of religious tolerance, subordination of Church to State, representative democracy, separation of powers, federalism, reduction of the armed forces, settlement of virgin lands with foreigners, small property owners, advancement of science, more schools, and the tutelage of the United States of America. According to one of their ideologists, the neighbor to the north should guide the destiny of Mexico "not only in its institutions, but also in its civil practices." All Liberals agreed on the ends, but not on the means. Some wanted to "go quickly," to fulfil the aspirations of Liberalism at all cost and as soon as possible; others wanted to "go slowly," to achieve the same ideals at less cost and without haste. The former were called *"puros"* or "reds" and the latter "moderates," and while *puros* and moderates argued with each other, the Conservatives took power.

José María Blancarte, a husky manufacturer of hats from Guadalajara, was disporting himself in the house of one-eyed Ruperta when he committed the crime of killing a policeman and thereafter he became successively a fugitive from justice, the man responsible for the fall of the governor of Jalisco, and the pronouncer of three revolutionary plans. The last, The Plan of the Hospicio, made three demands: removal from office of President Arista; a federal constitution; and recall of Santa Anna. With these demands he won the support of many local rebels, the Church hierarchy, the large landholders, and the leader of the Conservative Party, Alamán. At that time Alamán was very much in the public eye because of the publication of the last volume of his *Historia de México*, in which he maintained that Antonio López de Santa Anna, although worthless as a soldier, had the "energy and courage to govern" and that he could found a lasting and stable regime. "The law-abiding, responsible, and serious people" called Santa Anna out of exile and on April 1, 1853, he arrived at the port of Veracruz, reaching the capital on the 20th where he was received with decorated balconies, bells tolling, poetry recitations, and numerous other demonstrations of joy. The next day he formed a cabinet headed by Lucas Alamán. On April 22, Alamán abolished the provincial legislatures and created a new Ministry of Development, Colonization, Industry, and Commerce. On the 25th, the Lares Law prohibited the printing of "subversive, seditious, immoral, insulting, and slanderous writing," and the Liberals fell victims to dismissal, exile, and imprisonment.

With the death of Alamán on June 2, Santa Anna lost what had sustained him. After a talk with the slave-owner Gadsden, who had been sent by the United States government to acquire territories in the north, he sold La Mesilla of Arizona. But that was not the worst of his follies. He gave himself the title "His Most Supreme Highness"; imposed taxes on coaches, horses, dogs, and windows; gave banquets with imported princes; and organized lavish balls and ceremonies in his honor as well as huge orgies. Exulting in his extravagances, the one-footed president was unaware of the tempests that were rising against him both within and outside the country. A French adventurer, Count Raousset de Boulbon, invaded Sonora, which he planned to convert into a paradise lost; and apparently the pirate Walker had the same expectations for Baja California. Apaches and Comanches increased their depredations. The country suffered a new epidemic of bubonic plague. Many local chieftains, made unhappy by some of the centralist measures, began to plot conspiracies. The caudillo became increasingly deaf, surrounded by an army that reached 90,000 men, adulated by a swarm of sycophants, engrossed in cockfights and ceremonies.

The personalist government of Santa Anna damaged the prestige of the principles and men of the Conservative Party, while it strengthened the appeal of the Liberal Party whose members waited in New Orleans and Brownsville for the right moment to return to Mexico. The moment came at the beginning of 1854.

The president was at a ball when he received word that, in the village of Ayutla on March 1, 1854, Colonel Florencio Villarreal had pronounced a plan demanding that the dictator be deposed and a constitutional congress be convened. Charged with carrying out the plan was Juan Álvarez, an old and respected cacique (boss) of the "roughriders of the south." Colonel Ignacio Comonfort supported and modified the plan in Acapulco. To the original text he added a paragraph that demonstrated the presence of not only the *puros* but also the moderate group in the rebel movement. President Santa Anna, at the head of an army of 5,000 men, was roundly defeated by the rebels and furtively left the country in August 1855. A junta of insurgents named General Álvarez as interim president and he governed for a few months with a cabinet of five *puros*: the philosopher and scientist, Melchor Ocampo; the reformist, Ponciano Arriaga; the poet, Guillermo Prieto; the lawyer, Benito Juárez; and the economist, Miguel Lerdo de Tejada. The only "moderate" was the Minister Ignacio Comonfort, to whom General Álvarez turned over the presidency. Although the new president proceeded cautiously in implementing the Liberal reforms, not a day passed that his government did not face Conservative protests over the Juárez Law that restricted Church privileges, the Lerdo Law that disentailed properties owned by civil and religious corporations, and the Iglesias Law that prohibited the Church from controlling cemeteries and collecting parish taxes from the poor. Meanwhile, a Congress had been convened and, after election of its members, began work in 1856.

In the Constituent Congress called by the revolutionaries of Ayutla, the *puros* were in the majority and they included such distinguished intellectuals as Ponciano Arriaga, José María Mata, Melchor Ocampo, Ignacio Ramírez, and Francisco Zarco. A committee directed by Arriaga drafted a constitution, which was concluded and sworn to in February 1857. Basically, it followed the lines set down by the Constitution of 1824—a federal form of state and a republican, representative, and democratic form of government. Its innovations consisted in opening the way to government intervention in acts of public worship and Church discipline, elimination of the vice-presidency, and broadening of individual liberties. Freedom of education, industry, trade, labor, and the right of association were guaranteed. Comonfort, confirmed as president of the Republic, should have put into effect the new political document, but he did not. The Conservatives, led by General Félix Zuloaga, pronounced the Plan of Tacubaya demanding repeal of the Constitution. Efforts of the president to conciliate supporters of the Plan of Tacubaya were in vain, and the Conservatives recognized Zuloaga as president. Benito Juárez, Minister of the Supreme Court, who was next in line for the presidency, assumed the title and declared constitutional order restored.

After January 1858, the Liberal and Conservative Parties engaged in a war that in its first phase lasted three years. The first year the Conservatives triumphed. Generals Osollo, Márquez, Mejía, and Miramón—all career officers with disciplined troops—repeatedly defeated the forces of such inexperienced generals as Santos Degollado, Ignacio Zaragoza, and Jesús González Ortega. Juárez had to transfer his government to Guadalajara, where he was taken prisoner. Once freed, he left the country for several months and re-entered Mexico through the port of Veracruz, where he installed his Liberal Government. In the second year battles were won by both sides. In Veracruz, Juárez was attacked by the army of Miguel Miramón, who had been declared president of the Republic in February by the victorious Conservatives. Leonardo Márquez, the other outstanding Conservative general, conquered Santos Degollado in Tacubaya and baptized the latter "General Defeat," at the same time earning for himself the no less lugubrious title of "The Tiger of Tacubaya" for his massacre of the wounded and medical personnel.

Ignacio Ramírez expressed Liberal indignation in verse: "War without truce or rest, war on our enemies, until the day that detestable, impious race will find not even a tomb in the wrathful earth." Benito Juárez expressed it in laws—a half-dozen provisions called the "Reform Laws." Issued in July 1858, they called for nationalization of Church properties; the closing of monasteries and convents; the establishment of civil registry for certificates of birth, marriage, and death; the secularization of cemeteries; and the suppression of many religious festivals.

After Miramón was defeated in Silao and Calpulalpan, González Ortega entered Mexico City at the head of 30,000 men on January 1, 1861; Juárez and his cabinet followed on January 11. He forthwith expelled the Papal Nuncio, Archbishop Garza,

and several bishops, together with the diplomatic representatives of Spain, Guatemala, and Ecuador, countries that had
sided with the Conservatives. The latter, who continued to
maintain battle forces all over the country, embarked on the
"synthetic war," which consisted in hunting down and shooting
the leading figures of Liberalism. Ocampo, Degollado, and Valle
were victims of this war.

While Conservative guerrilla fighters pursued Liberals, Conservative political leaders negotiated in Europe for the establishment and support of a second empire. Financial difficulties had
compelled the Liberal Government to suspend payment of its
foreign debt and interest. England, Spain, and France protested
against this measure and in the London Convention of October
1861 they agreed to intervene in Mexico to secure payment of the
debt by force. The French imperial couple, Napoleon and Eugénie,
who furthermore wished to raise a monarchical and Latin barrier
against United States expansion, became involved with the
Mexican Conservatives. The moment was ripe; half of the United
States fought against the other half in the Civil War, and they could
not help the Liberals. The first interventionist troops landed in
Veracruz between December 1861 and January 1862. The Liberal
Government entered into negotiations with them and, through the
Treaties of La Soledad, arranged for withdrawal of the English and
Spanish armies.

France remained alone and determined to impose a monarchy
on Mexico with the support of a large and disciplined expeditionary force and the remains of the troops of the Conservative Party.
The French army was commanded successively by Lorencez, Forey,
and Bazaine. The first-mentioned was repulsed outside of Puebla
on May 5 and this initial engagement united the great majority of
the Mexican people against the French. The second destroyed the
Liberal army, took possession of the capital, and appointed a
governing junta to elect members of an Assembly of Notables and
a provisional executive body. The third—while the "Notables," in
complicity with Napoleon III, offered the crown of the Mexican
Empire to Ferdinand Maximilian of Hapsburg—campaigned
throughout the country, obliging Juárez to establish his government in Paso del Norte, a step from the United States border.

Maximilian accepted the crown. Under the Convention of Miramar, he undertook to pay to Napoleon III the substantial sum of 260 000 000 francs for expenses of the French intervention; and he reached the shores of Mexico on May 28, 1864. Maximilian, Archduke of Austria, married to the beautiful Belgian princess Charlotte, was a romantic who loved nature, firmly believed in the goodness of the Noble Savage and in liberal ideology. Therefore, he ended by disconcerting the Conservatives who had brought him to Mexico. Convinced that "the great majority of Mexicans were liberal and demanded a program of progress in the truest sense of the word," he endorsed the Laws of the Reform. He required an official pass for papal documents; decreed religious tolerance and nationalization of Church properties; secularized cemeteries; established a civil registry; issued laws on wages and work conditions, pensions and pawnhouses; and established a decimal system of weights and measures. He became so reformist that the Papal Nuncio left in a rage and the Liberals laughed to see how the crabs had been fooled: "It has always been the custom of crabs to maneuver by moving backward, which is contrary to common sense. But suddenly Juárez appears and he tells them: crabs, you must go forward. Raving mad and shouting insults, they go backward across the ocean to look for someone to avenge them ... they find that all their plans go up in smoke and that the very ones who were supposed to avenge them, make them furious by saying firmly: crabs, you must go forward."

However, the imperial laws were never enforced. At the end of the Civil War, the United States demanded the departure of the French. Meanwhile, the French emperor was obliged by the threat of Prussia to recall his troops from Mexico. Without the European army, Maximilian could not hold out against the Liberal armies under Mariano Escobedo, Ramón Corona, and Porfirio Díaz. He surrendered in Querétaro on May 15, 1867 and, together with Generals Miramón and Mejía, was executed on a small hill known as the Cerro de las Campanas on June 19.

Bibliography

BARKER, Nancy Nichols. *The French Experience in Mexico, 1821-1861. A History of Constant Misunderstanding*. Chapel Hill, University of North Carolina Press, 1979.

BASCH, S. *Memoirs of Mexico. A History of the Last Ten Months of the Empire*. Translated by Hugh McAden Oechler. San Antonio, Trinity University Press, 1973.

BRACK, Gene M. *Mexico Views Manifest Destiny, 1821-1846: An Essay on the Origins of the Mexican War*. Albuquerque, University of New Mexico Press, 1976.

BROWN, Charles H. *Agents of Manifest Destiny: The Lives and Times of the Filibusters*. Chapel Hill, University of North Carolina Press, 1980.

CALDERÓN DE LA BARCA, Frances Erskine. *Life in Mexico: The Letters of Fanny Calderón de la Barca*. Garden City, New Jersey, Doubleday, 1970.

COATSWORTH, John H. *Growth Against Development: The Economic Impact of Railroads in Porfirian Mexico*. De Kalb, Northern Illinois University Press, 1981.

COERVER, Don M. *The Porfirian Interregnum: The Presidency of Manuel González of Mexico, 1880-1884*. Fort Worth, Texas Christian University Press, 1979.

CONNOR, Seymour and Odie B. FAULK. *North America Divided. The Mexican War 1846-1848*. Oxford, Oxford University Press, 1971.

COSTELOE, Michael P. *Church and State in Independent Mexico: A Study of the Patronage Debate, 1821-1857*. London, Royal Historical Society, 1978.

FLETCHER, David H. *The Diplomacy of Annexation: Texas, Oregon, and the Mexican War*. Columbia, University of Missouri Press, 1974.

LANDER, Ernest M. Jr. *Reluctant Imperialists: Calhoun, the South Carolinians, and the Mexican War*. Baton Rouge, Louisiana State University Press, 1980.

OLLIFF, Donathon C. *Reforma Mexico and the United States: A Search for Alternatives to Annexation, 1854-1861*. Alabama, University of Alabama Press, 1981.

PARKERS, Morris B. *Mules, Mines, and Me in Mexico, 1895-1932*. Edited by James M. Day. Tucson, University of Arizona Press, 1979.

PERRY, Laurens Ballard. *Juárez and Díaz; Machine Politics in Mexico*. De Kalb, Northern Illinois University Press, 1978.

PRICE, Glenn W. *Origins of the War with Mexico. The Polk-Stockton Intrigue*. Austin, University of Texas Press, 1976.

SCHOONOVER, Thomas David. *Dollar over Dominion: The Triumph of Liberalism in Mexican-United States Relations, 1861-1867.* Baton Rouge, Louisiana State University Press, 1978.

SIERRA, Justo. *The Political Evolution of the Mexican People.* Translated by Charles Ramsdell. Austin, University of Texas Press, 1969.

VANDENDWOOD, Paul. *Disorder and Progress: Bandits, Police, and Mexican Development.* Lincoln, University of Nebraska Press, 1981.

IV. THE MODERN SPAN

Daniel Cosío Villegas

1

THE RESTORED REPUBLIC

THE MODERN HISTORY of Mexico begins and ends with a downfall. It begins in July 1867, when the Empire of Maximilian is overthrown, and it concludes in May 1911, when the government of Porfirio Díaz is deposed. This history therefore embraces forty-four years which, nonetheless, are usually divided into two periods. The initial period of only ten years goes from 1867 to 1876 and is called the Restored Republic. The second, covering the thirty-four years from 1877 to 1911, is called the Porfiriato. The first name is justified because the Empire of Maximilian tried to put an end to the Republic of Juárez and when the latter, after five long and anguished years, triumphed, the victors insisted that the victorious Republic was the same one, only restored; that is, "placed in the state or position that it had had before." The name Porfiriato is self-explanatory; it means that the period was so dominated by the figure of Porfirio Díaz that it ended by taking his name.

The victory of the Republic over the Empire and of the Liberal Party over the Conservative seemed to open to Mexico the paradise that had been dreamed of since the Grito de Dolores launched the Independence movement. The defeat of foreign intervention relieved Mexico of outside pressures, including that of the United States, which by taking the side of the Republic had become its friend and ally. The political and military victory of the Liberal over the Conservative group signified the end of bitter disputes that frequently led to the battlefield. It seemed that for the first time in its long and stormy history, Mexico was free of external and internal ambushes and that it would enjoy the peace and tranquility it needed to devote all its time and efforts to banishing poverty and reviving its economy through development of its abundant natural resources.

This prospect appeared even more certain because the executive, legislative, and judicial branches of the government comprised the most experienced and patriotic group in the nation's history. Benito Juárez was the president of the Republic, and his chief ministers were Sebastián Lerdo de Tejada, José María Iglesias, and Matías Romero. Sebastián Lerdo de Tejada was intelligent and cultured, first a student and later professor and director of the famous San Ildefonso College; he had already been a federal deputy, but he gained prominence as companion and advisor to Juárez in the pilgrimage of the Republic that concluded in Paso del Norte. Another member of the so-called "Trinity" of Paso del Norte was the distinguished lawyer, José María Iglesias, an honest and stern man who held the Ministries of Justice, Interior, and Finance, in addition to presiding over the Supreme Court. In the Supreme Court were figures of the stature of Ignacio Ramírez, writer, journalist, and an outstanding deputy in the Constituent Congress of 1856; and the eminent constitutionalists Ezequiel Montes, José María Lafragua, and José María Castillo Velasco. Among the deputies were Francisco Zarco, famous chronicler of that same Constituent Congress, who has become the patron saint of Mexican journalists, as well as Manuel Payno, popular writer and authority on public finance, and Manuel María de Zamacona, notable journalist and brilliant orator.

Nevertheless, powerful forces firmly entrenched in the national soil were going to stand in the way of these good intentions and illustrious men. The continual civil and foreign wars had created an attitude of intolerance in the Mexican, who had reached the extreme of believing that he could not settle a political dispute without physically eliminating his adversary, whether by felling him on the battlefield or exiling him. The last two wars of the Reform and of the Empire had produced a generous crop of "heroes" who claimed from the government and from society itself power, wealth, and honors as compensation for what they considered to be invaluable services rendered to the fatherland. These wars also left behind 80 000 to 100 000 uprooted soldiers who, having tasted adventure and the power of holding a rifle, refused to return to their badly paid and routine work in the countryside or city. The national economy, which had always been a primitive one based on a subsistence agriculture and on silver and gold mining, had been destroyed by ten years of perpetual warfare. Therefore, it could not absorb these rootless soldiers, much less offer them a stable employment that would give them any hope of living better than before.

Although Conservatives and Liberals had left off quarrelling they soon began to split into personalist factions that fought each other with the same fury, but no longer with the justification that they fought for ideas. In the first presidential election of 1867, it was the Juárez faction against that of Porfirio Díaz; in the second election of 1871, the contest was between these two factions plus that of Sebastián Lerdo de Tejada; after the death of Juárez in 1872, his faction was replaced by that of José María Iglesias; and in 1876 the latter disputed the presidency with supporters of Lerdo and Díaz.

The Constitution of 1857 still embodied the faith and hope of the Liberals. Because its promulgation had unleashed the War of the Reform, and the Intervention had tried to suppress the republican form of government, the early years of the Restored Republic engendered an exalted sentiment of constitutionalism that required those in authority to adhere strictly to the text of the Magna Carta. But this sentiment was not entirely shared by the rulers of the country, in particular Juárez and Lerdo de Tejada. They believed that for the era of reconstruction ahead, the Restored Republic would need a powerful executive branch to neutralize a deliberating assembly such as the single chamber of deputies created by the Constitution.

Finally, as occurs with any great social upheaval, the Wars of the Reform and Intervention had accelerated the maturing of young men. Without passing through the long and painful stages of apprenticeship, they had assumed positions of authority during the war and they were not prepared to give up this authority just because the country had returned to peace. Thus began an intergenerational conflict not so much due to differences in age or education as to a different vision of life in general and of the country in particular.

Well aware of the tremendous problems facing the Restored Republic, the ruling group rapidly took the actions they thought would be most effective. In order to revive the economy, President Juárez did not hesitate to expose himself to public criticism by renewing the concession of an English company to resume work immediately on Mexico's first railway. On completion, this railway would join the capital, the center of the national nervous system, with Veracruz, at that time the only port which connected Mexico with the outside world and through which all international trade was conducted. Juárez based this measure on his debatable use of the extraordinary powers granted him by Congress to cope with the French intervention. And he took this step despite the laws of war he himself had drafted which imposed automatic cancellation of any concession given to enterprises or individuals who had dealt with the imperialist authorities.

Barely a month after he had installed his government in the capital, Juárez held general elections for the president of the Republic, federal deputies, and judges of the Supreme Court, so that the country could recover as soon as possible a normal constitutional life. In 1867 all the authorities of the country, from the president of the Republic down to the last village mayor, were de facto authorities—that is, not legally designated or elected. For the purpose of reestablishing the balance between the executive and legislative powers, Juárez and Lerdo wanted to take advantage of the elections of August 1867 to submit the necessary constitutional reforms to a popular plebiscite.

Not forgetting the inter-generational conflict, President Juárez soon appointed thirty-three year old Ignacio Vallarta to be Minister of Interior. He also reorganized the army and reduced it to five divisions of 4,000 men each, thus demobilizing another 4,000 soldiers and officers.

Although these and other measures were certainly correct, they were inadequate.

It took six years to finish the Mexican railway and when it began to operate in 1873, it was discovered that whereas it certainly revived imports and exports, it did little or nothing to develop the domestic economy. What Mexico actually needed was a network of railways and another of roads to service the areas not reached by the railways; and this required an enormous investment of capital, which Mexico did not have. Nor was it possible to seek foreign capital because, as a consequence of the War of Intervention, Mexico had broken its diplomatic relations with England, France, and Spain, the only countries where it could have obtained such capital. And as though this were not enough, Mexico had no credit in the international capital markets because since 1824 it had been in arrears in payment of its foreign debts.

The constitutional reforms advocated by Juárez and Lerdo failed because the procedure of a popular plebiscite was unconstitutional. They then proposed the creation of a senate to serve as a counterbalance to the single chamber of deputies and it was approved, but not until six years later.

The appointment of young Vallarta did not resolve the intergenerational conflict, partly because Vallarta had mistakenly understood that Juárez had picked him to replace Lerdo de Tejada, but mainly because Juárez decided to reelect himself in 1871, and Lerdo intended to become president in 1876. Once the young men saw their access to public life closed off by older men, they believed that the only road left was to rebel against them or to wait patiently for them to die.

Most serious of all, however, was the guerrilla spirit of the "heroes" who—sometimes on a flimsy pretext and sometimes for reasons that could have been discussed and settled reasonably—organized a series of military uprisings against Presidents Juárez and Lerdo that plunged the country back into the anguish and misery of civil war.

As a result of all this, the country longed for order, tranquility, and peace, and no less for an end to the poverty in which it had lived for more than half a century.

2

THE PORFIRIATO

THE PERIOD FROM 1877 TO 1911 is called the Porfiriato because the figure of Porfirio Díaz dominated it, although not from the first day. That figure had taken shape over the previous ten years and it barely reached full stature in 1888.

On July 15, 1867, Juárez entered the capital to receive the popular acclaim celebrating the republican victory; the same day, Porfirio Díaz announced his decision to retire from the army and to dedicate himself to his hacienda, La Noria, near the city of Oaxaca. This decision was applauded, for it was unusual that one of the great leaders of the war against the Empire should renounce voluntarily such a high position for the life of a simple farmer. Three months later he ran against Juárez in the presidential election of December 1867.

This was a clear portent of the firmness with which Díaz would enter political life. He did not hesitate to state his intention of ascending in one leap to the highest position of the country, even though his background hardly seemed to warrant such an ambition. His education had been deficient and truncated; he had had absolutely no experience in administration and politics; and he was challenging Juárez, the most mature politician and statesman, who at that moment had reached the zenith of his glory.

Although Juárez won the election, it was significant that Porfirio received almost a third of the total vote and, as candidate for the presidency of the Supreme Court, 42 percent of the vote, against Sebastián Lerdo de Tejada.

Porfirio returned to La Noria, but not exactly to cultivate his fields. He soon sought to be elected governor of the states of Morelos and Mexico as well as federal deputy. Failing in the first two attempts, he won in the third, so that for the first time in his life and at the not very early age of thirty-eight years, he held an elected post. Uneducated, lacking any ideology, inarticulate, he was a pigmy next to the greatest parliamentarians in the history of the country, most of whom were, moreover, his political opponents because they belonged to the Juárez group. Díaz was slow to occupy his bench and slower still to make his first speech, which came out so badly that he decided never to return to the chamber of deputies.

Anyone but Porfirio Díaz would have been discouraged after three political defeats and his poor showing in the parliamentary test. In the next presidential election of 1871, he again ran against Juárez and Sebastián Lerdo de Tejada. No one obtained an absolute majority and therefore, under the constitution, Congress had to choose between the candidates who had received the most votes. Juárez, who was in first place and who had a majority in Congress, was elected.

Porfirio was incapable of appreciating the significance of this episode. It meant that the popularity of Juárez had declined so sharply that he had fallen from two-thirds of the vote to less than half. On the other hand, the popularity of Porfirio had grown to the extent that he won more votes than Sebastián Lerdo de Tejada, who was a consummate statesman—talented, cultured, and experienced. Furthermore, Porfirio was unlucky in that Juárez died seven months after beginning his new term. Elections would have been held immediately and Díaz could have repeated his recent triumph over Lerdo, the only other possible candidate. Then he would have reached the presidency, not in 1877 as actually occurred, but five years earlier; and he would have reached it pacifically and democratically.

The truth is that Porfirio, convinced that Juárez would seek reelection, forestalled this sequence of events by attempting to seize power by arms. His disaster could not have been more complete or more resounding. Militarily, despite his following of local caudillos with experience and resources, he was defeated by the government forces in battle after battle. Politically, the revolt, which had been mounted against reelection of the president, lost its motive when Juárez died on July 18, 1872. Taking advantage of this double circumstance, the interim president offered amnesty to the rebels with no more penalty than the loss of their military rank and honors.

Although Porfirio refused the amnesty as humiliating, he was subsequently taken by surprise with only a few men by the rural police of Chihuahua, and he had to surrender. After a solitary passage through Mexico City, ignored by his friends who neither welcomed him nor sought him out, he hurried on to Tlacotalpan, where he opened a carpenter's workshop. Three years later, anticipating that Lerdo de Tejada would seek reelection in July 1876, Porfirio again took up arms. This time he was lucky, for he triumphed over the government forces in the battle of Tecoac in November of that year. After years of struggle, he finally came to power; but his victory did not save him from a series of calamities.

The first was that—notwithstanding his having made himself constitutional president on May 5, 1877, through elections that had every appearance of legality—the United States refused to recognize his government unless it met certain requirements. Lack of this recognition posed an immediate and direct threat to the government of Díaz, because the United States could foment movements against it by selling arms and munitions to supporters of the deposed President Lerdo, now exiled in Texas.

Not all the calamities came from abroad; some were internal. The country was horrified by the activities of the "Tuxtepecos," the name given to the partisans of Díaz because the revolt had been carried out under the aegis of the Plan of Tuxtepec. Driven by an irrational hatred of Lerdo de Tejada, they formed "Committees of Public Health" to denounce the *Lerdista* sympathies of public employees and even of private individuals and corporations. They demanded dismissal of the former and confiscation of the property of the latter. Still not satisfied, they tried to take over the municipal councils of the Federal District, without having regard for the political commitments of their revolutionary chief.

The immediate collaborators of Porfirio made a good impression. Protasio Tagle was Minister of the Interior; Ignacio L. Vallarta, of Foreign Relations; Justo Benítez, of Finance; Ignacio

Ramírez, of Justice; Vicente Riva Palacio, of Development; and Pedro Ogazón, of War. But except for Vallarta and Ogazón, who had both governed Jalisco, none of the others had any political-administrative experience. Therefore, Porfirio and his colleagues were bound together only by a vague sensation that the affairs of the country were going badly and that they had to be straightened out in some way. However, they not only had no clear idea of how to improve the situation but they did not even realize that the Tuxtepec revolt had had two important consequences: a generation of experienced and patriotic governors had disappeared and had been succeeded by a generation of political parvenus. Furthermore, the old generation had possessed a vision of the life and problems of the country, a vision which the new generation rejected, without presenting another to replace it.

For lack of ideas, Porfirio substituted action, which in any event suited his temperament. For example, he bent all his efforts to getting out of Congress an authorization for new railways and he obtained it barely a month before leaving the presidency in November 1880. His successor, General Manuel González, was therefore able to go ahead with construction of the Central Railway linking the capital with Ciudad Juárez and of the National Railway from the capital to Nuevo Laredo. In his subsequent governments, Díaz himself continued this program so that at the end of the Porfiriato, Mexico had progressed from a single railway of 287 miles in 1877, to a complete railway grid of almost 12 000 miles. At the same time, postal, telegraph, and even telephone communications spread out to cover a large part of the national territory. Work on port facilities was carried out in Veracruz, Tampico, and Salina Cruz. Later in the Porfiriato, a number of banks were created that made possible the expansion of agriculture, mining, commerce, and industry. In short, the development of the country's overall economy was of an unprecedented degree and scope.

The formula that best expressed the concept Porfirio had of governing and, naturally, of his own mission was the well-known "little politics, much administration," which in time turned into "zero politics, one hundred percent administration." As brief and simple as this slogan appeared, it said everything.

First, the president of the Republic would determine the most suitable direction for the country to take, as well as the best means to overcome obstacles in the way. Second, senators and deputies should approve whatever the president proposed because they lacked the technical information that the cabinet ministers gave to the president and because the president had no other desire than to serve the country disinterestedly. Third, public opinion and the people had to have confidence in the ability and patriotism of the president and to renew this confidence when they were benefitted by the fruits of his action. Fourth, the formula meant that open public confrontation of opposing interests, opinions, and sentiments would be sterile; that only presidential action would be fertile, always directed toward material progress and to maintaining order and peace as its necessary condition.

"Little politics and much administration" functioned satisfactorily for many years because the country yearned for peace and wanted to improve its economic condition and because Porfirio showed that he could maintain peace and that he knew how to promote the national economy. However, he became increasingly oppressive until he finally provoked the Madero rebellion.

No egalitarian society has ever existed which distributed its wealth in exactly equal proportions among all its members. But the unequal distribution of Mexico's new wealth seemed much more striking and this could only be explained by the insatiable appetite of the rich to become ever richer at the expense, of course, of the poor, who should have been treated as brothers.

In the latter part of the past century, just as today, there were a couple of countries—England and the United States—which were notoriously prosperous; following them, although at a good distance, came a somewhat more numerous group—France, Germany, and Holland; and lagging far behind were the rest of the countries and regions of the world. Such a strange phenomenon required an explanation, which was furnished by what was called liberalism. This philosophy recognized that in all nations, without exception, society was a pyramid with a few very wealthy people on top, a larger collection of medium-income people halfway up, and a great mass of poor at the necessarily much broader base. It argued that the rain of wealth that fell on the peak of this social structure trickled downward, making the whole pyramid fruitful, until it reached the strata of the poor. Thanks to the benefits they received from the fertilizing rain, the latter could leave their condition of poverty to climb first to the middle of the pyramid and finally to scale its height and become rich.

This idea, largely confirmed by the experience of the United States and England, was inoperative in Mexico for two good reasons. First, Mexico's social pyramid was not, as in those countries, tall with a narrow base so that the fertilizing water drained down an almost vertical slope. In Mexico the pyramid was squat with a very broad base so that the flow was slow and almost horizontal. More important, separating each of the three layers of the Mexican pyramid was a thick impermeable slab, like concrete, that caused rainfall to stagnate on the crest with little or no flow to the lower sections of the pyramid.

Social mobility in the Mexican society of that time was so limited that it was a miracle that Benito Juárez, beginning as a poor ignorant Indian, had risen to the pinnacle of power and fame. He who was born poor and a nobody usually died in the same condition. Although passing from the lower layer to the middle or upper layers was difficult in the economic and social spheres, it was even more difficult in the strictly political sphere.

Gradually overcoming such obstacles was a new generation of young men who had graduated as lawyers, doctors, or engineers and who were eager to participate, make a career, distinguish themselves in public life. They wanted to be officials in the bureaucracy, to be congressmen or judges, to be active in education and journalism; but they found these posts filled from time immemorial by old men and these old men seemed to live forever. The young men did not notice that there were few posts within the government and fewer still in what today would be called private enterprise. They believed that Mexican society was completely petrified and that unless they themselves did something to shatter it, they would never occupy a place in it.

This was exactly what happened in the last elections of the Porfiriato, when for the first time in thirty-three years various political parties were formed. Although opposition candidates ran for deputies and senators in July 1910, not one of them won a seat in Congress. As for the presidential elections, these same parties would have reelected Porfirio Díaz once more if he had permitted free election of the vice-president; but he disregarded this fair and reasonable request and imposed the reelectionist formula of Porfirio Díaz-Ramón Corral.

With all doors closed against him Francisco I. Madero decided to launch an armed rebellion on November 20, 1910, and within six months a system of government that had remained in power for thirty-four years collapsed.

Bibliography

ANDERSON, Rodney Dean. *Outcasts in Their Own Land: Mexican Industrial Workers, 1906-1911.* De Kalb, Northern Illinois University Press, 1976.

BRADING, D. A., ed. *Caudillo and Peasant in the Mexican Revolution.* Cambridge, Cambridge University Press, 1980.

CALVERT, Peter. *The Mexican Revolution (1910-1914). The Diplomacy of the Anglo American Conflict.* Cambridge, Cambridge University Press,1968.

CLARK, Marjorie Ruth. *Organized Labor in Mexico.* Chapel Hill, University of North Carolina Press, 1934.

COATSWORTH, John H. *Growth against Development. The Economic Impact of Railroads in Porfirian Mexico.* De Kalb, Northern Illinois University Press, 1981.

COCKCROFT, James D. *Intellectual Precursors of the Mexican Revolution, 1900-1913.* Austin, University of Texas Press, 1976.

CUMBERLAND, Charles C. *The Mexican Revolution. The Constitutional Year.* Austin, University of Texas Press, 1972.

DULLES, John. *Yesterday in Mexico: A Chronicle of the Revolution,1919-1936.* Austin, University of Texas Press, 1961.

GILDERHUS, Mark T. *Diplomacy and Revolution; U.S.-Mexican Relations under Wilson and Carranza.* Tucson, University of Arizona Press, 1977.

HALL, Linda. *Álvaro Obregón: Power and Revolution in Mexico, 1910-1920.* College Station, Texas A & M University Press, 1981.

HART, John M. *Anarchism and the Mexican Working Class, 1860-1931.* Austin, University of Texas Press, 1978.

HENDERSON, Peter V. N. *Félix Díaz, the Porfirians, and the Mexican Revolution.* Lincoln, University of Nebraska Press, 1981.

KATZ, Friedrich. *The Secret War in Mexico, Europe, the United States, and the Mexican Revolution.* Portions translated by Loren Goldner. Chicago, University of Chicago Press, 1981.

LEVY, Daniel. *University and Government in Mexico: Autonomy in an Authoritarian System.* New York, Praeger Publishers, 1980.

MEYER, Jean. *The Cristero Rebellion: The Mexican People Between Church and State, 1926-1929.* Cambridge, Cambridge University Press, 1976.

POOLE, David, ed. *Land and Liberty: Anarchist Influences in the Mexican Revolution: Ricardo Flores Magón.* Sanday, Orkney, England, Cienfuegos Press, 1977.

QUIRK, Robert E. *Mexican Revolution, 1914-1915: The Convention of Aguascalientes.* Westport, Conn., Greenwood Press, 1981.

REED, John. *Insurgent Mexico.* New York, Simon and Schuster, 1974.

ROSS, Stanley, ed. *Is the Mexican Revolution Dead?* New York, A. Knopf, 1966.

WHITECOTTON, Joseph W. *The Zapotecs: Princes, Priests, and Peasants.* Norman, University of Oklahoma Press,1977.
WOLFSKILL, George Douglas and W. RICHMOND, eds. *Essays on the Mexican Revolution: Revisionist Views of the Leaders.* Austin, University of Texas Press, 1979.
WOMACK, John. *Zapata and the Mexican Revolution.* New York, A. Knopf, 1968.

V. THE MEXICAN REVOLUTION

Eduardo Blanquel

1

1910-1920

THE MEXICAN REVOLUTION, like any historical event, varied with the passage of time and was complex in its organization and development. It arose as a clearly political protest against the Porfirian regime; but those who participated in it left the imprint of their ideas, interests, and aspirations.

In 1910 Porfirio Díaz had himself reelected president of Mexico for the sixth consecutive time. Over thirty years of a power that steadily increased but did little to renew its men and methods had resulted in the paradox of an undeniably strong present and, at the same time, an imminent weakness. Although nothing and no one appeared to be capable of discussing the Porfiriato, still less of replacing it, it was already threatened by its manifest ageing and by the ever closer possibility of the death of the caudillo. At the time of what was to be his last reelection, General Díaz was eighty years old. For all these reasons, since 1904 Mexico had been faced with the problem of who would replace the president. By lengthening his presidential term from four to six years, Díaz put off the problem, but he did not eliminate it.

In 1908 President Díaz gave an interview to the American journalist, James Creelman. He described himself as the last of the indispensable men in the history of Mexico. His long tenure in power and his stern exercise of that power had made it possible—he said—to bring about an essential change in the political and social organization of the country; he had shortened, almost to the point of abolishing, the distance that existed between an advanced constitutional law and a people without political education. Díaz believed that his legitimate successor—the only one possible—would emerge from the organization of Mexicans into true political parties, from a free and open electoral contest. The Mexican people, said Porfirio Díaz, were now ready for democracy.

Many took the words of the president literally, and a climate of true debate, unknown in the country for some time, was produced. Numerous publications and politicians expressed their views. Soon, however, two currents of ideas clearly appeared. On the one hand, were those who possessed social and economic influence without political power and who hoped to be the natural heirs of the Porfiriato; as the step following the personalist government of Porfirio Díaz and previous to a democratic government, they advocated a kind of oligarchy that would be intellectual and—very much in the style of the period—scientific. On the other, were those who stood for an orthodox liberalism based on the belief that all people had an inherent capacity for democratic life; they thought that the Mexican, exercising his electoral right, would bring to power the person who should govern, and deserved to govern, the country.

In this last line of thought was Francisco I. Madero, a man who was keenly interested in and concerned with political questions. In 1908 he had published a book, *La sucesión presidencial en 1910* (The Presidential Succession in 1910). More important, Madero and Díaz both thought that Mexico already had a real and numerous middle class capable of assuming political responsibilities. From the perspective of his own social background, Madero inevitably concluded that the Mexican people were ready for democracy. Therefore, he urged them to organize into parties and begin an authentic institutional life. This was the only way to guarantee peace and to safeguard the continuity of government programs because—said Madero—men will perish, but institutions are immortal.

Nevertheless, in a gesture of conciliatory realism and no doubt thinking that a total rupture of the national political system would not be easy, Madero proposed that the immediate election be only for a vice-president. The latter would thus learn how to govern so that, when Díaz disappeared from the political scene, he would naturally and smoothly occupy the place of command. Díaz did not respond to any of these propositions. Furthermore, when from the front ranks of the government Bernardo Reyes took tentative, even fearful, steps toward becoming candidate, he was abruptly forced out of national life.

Faced with these contradictions of what Díaz had said earlier, Madero went on to put his ideas into practice. After organizing an Anti-Reelectionist Party, he began an electoral campaign, something unprecedented in the entire history of Mexico. Accompanied only by his wife and a colleague as fellow speechmakers, Madero visited a large part of the country. The campaign of Madero aroused first ridicule, then alarm, and finally repression in government circles. The tiny figure of the man who dared to challenge Díaz, if only because he had taken that position, grew in stature with popular contact and he came to symbolize the little David so many Mexicans had waited for.

In June 1910 Madero contemplated the electoral process from the prison to which his boldness had taken him. Weeks earlier, the first disturbances in places as far apart as Yucatán and Sinaloa had reflected the mood of Mexico. On October 4, 1910, Congress declared Porfirio Díaz president, and Ramón Corral vice-president, for the next six years. On October 5 Madero, free on bond, crossed the border into the United States. The revolution loomed on the horizon.

From his refuge in Texas, Francisco I. Madero issued his revolutionary plan in which he denounced the June election as fraudulent, refused to recognize the constituted authorities, proclaimed himself provisional president until new elections, proposed to legally redress the abuses committed during the Porfiriato, and summoned the people to rebellion on November 20. These were the basic points of his Plan of San Luis Potosí, which were summed up in the slogan, "Effective Suffrage and No Reelection."

When the revolutionary conspiracy was discovered in Puebla on November 18, the movement suffered its first casualties in Aquiles Serdán and his companions. Not only that, but the fear of some revolutionaries, the watchful waiting of others, the insecurity of many, and even early disagreements made the initial days of the movement uncertain. Finally, thanks to the help of one of Mexico's regional and renowned patriarchal figures—Abraham González, the Chihuahua caudillo—Madero gained the support of Pascual Orozco and Francisco Villa, who would become his first military leaders. The revolution had begun.

The Díaz regime counterattacked and Chihuahua was to be the stage of its great defeats. Ciudad Guerrero, Mal Paso, Casas Grandes, Chihuahua, and Ciudad Juárez were the battles that paved the way of the revolution. Emiliano Zapata led an uprising in the south and there were insurrections in other parts of the country. Having failed militarily, Díaz resorted to negotiations while he tried to shore up his political edifice by changing officials. Nothing worked. Echoing the revolutionary victories in the north, there were mutinies against Díaz in the capital itself. The latter finally resigned and fled the country. After six months of struggle, the Madero revolution had triumphed.

The military victor, Madero, negotiated power through the Treaties of Ciudad Juárez by placing some of his men in the interim government. He waited for his mandate to have an unquestionably democratic origin and he was not mistaken. His arrival in Mexico City after his triumph was a spontaneous and authentic plebiscite which was legally formalized in the 1911 elections.

Although the interim presidency of Francisco León de la Barra could not be a restoration, it served to provoke new dissensions among the revolutionaries. Some had been frustrated in their pursuit of power, others thought compromise was betrayal of the revolution, and many succumbed to intrigues plotted by men of the old regime to divide the movement.

In these circumstances, Madero assumed power with a gravely splintered party, as was clearly demonstrated by the uprising of Emiliano Zapata under the Plan of Ayala scarcely twenty days after Madero had taken office. However, the defection of Zapata went far beyond the purely political to new and advanced ideas on what the objectives of the revolution should be. The slow history of Porfirian Mexico suddenly accelerated. Those who had been so long without land demanded that the lever of power, now in the hands of the revolutionary leaders, be used to satisfy them immediately.

But in addition to the fact that the armed revolt had not affected the social or economic organization of the Porfirian world, Madero had his own convictions on the meaning of the revolution. For him, a newly elected president, the solution to the major national problems should be found within the law, this being the only true road to follow. Everything had hitherto been done by force; now, even the most urgent needs, such as that of land, were to be met by rule of law.

Politically, Madero was to become the victim of his democratic zeal, which prevented him from understanding the need for a unilateral and monolithic government to consolidate his victory. The democratic game was begun too soon. Thus, the Twenty-Sixth Federal Legislature included as many emissaries from the Porfirian past as representatives of the revolutionary present. But whereas the former joined together as never before to defend themselves, each revolutionary was determined to take the movement along the path he judged to be best. Only a few with political vision like Luis Cabrera, Gustavo A. Madero, and Serapio Rendón tried in vain to give the revolution a strong government.

The national situation became more complex by the minute. Those who controlled economic power were deeply worried by the ferment, for their existence and prosperity depended on peace and security. If Madero was incapable of bringing order to the country, forceful action had to be taken against his government. Their alarm grew when the Mexican president dared to correct the illegal situation enjoyed by some foreign investors, thanks to which they were exempt from even such minimal obligations to the country as payment of taxes. Led by representatives of these foreign interests and with the United States Embassy as their headquarters, the Mexicans defeated by the revolution joined with the Porfirian army, which had survived almost intact. Their successful assault on the government ended in the assassination of Madero.

The regime of Victoriano Huerta always lacked a social base, not only because of the brutal way it had seized power but also because the presence of the opposing interests created by the revolution made a real restoration impossible. The Huerta government was ineffective in its historical moment despite the support of intellectuals and politicians who tried to give it principles and programs to respond to the problems of the time. Bound by origin and necessity to the international policy of the United States, Huerta was rejected when the latter changed course and he thenceforth had to keep himself in power by his own efforts.

After the death of Madero, the revolutionaries instinctively regrouped. With Venustiano Carranza as their caudillo, they set out to restore the constitutional order shattered by the Huerta coup. To the already famous names of Villa and Zapata were added others—Obregón and Pesqueira, Diéguez, Hill and Pablo González, Amaro, Gertrudis Sánchez, and Rómulo Figueroa. All united and with victories like Torreón, Orendain, and Tepic, they soon wore down the resistance of Huerta who, after committing many crimes and involving the country in serious international conflicts, finally relinquished power in 1914.

Carranza, the new chief, was a shrewd politician. Having learned the lessons of the immediate past, he dissolved the military machine inherited from the Porfiriato and devoted himself to consolidating a strong government, which—he said—would eventually make possible the needed social and economic changes. He also maintained that only revolutionary unity could withstand the pressures from abroad on national sovereignty.

For the moment, the Carranza program seemed correct and his success in international relations increased his prestige and power. But the revolution continually uncovered old and new grievances. Agrarian problems in certain parts of the country could not be postponed. The intensity of political debate was partly explained by all the previous years of enforced silence. The ambitions of the new caudillos, conscious of their popular and armed force, appeared to be limitless. Five years after the start of the revolution, the country was shown to be a human mosaic with needs so different and at times so at variance that they defied any possible form of true national organization.

The prolonged and growing power of Carranza was disputed by various groups of revolutionaries. Two conventions—one in Mexico City and another in Aguascalientes—were held in an attempt to resolve the problem of the leadership of the movement without resorting to violence. The results were contrary to expectations; this first confrontation of social and political ideas and positions separated the groups that gathered there more profoundly than ever.

Given the new panorama, Carranza had to govern more firmly and practice a crude politics with emphasis not on the application of general principles but on the ability to resolve even momentarily the most pressing social problems. Some of these problems would be dealt with by force of arms, others in the sphere of ideas, all in the midst of a new period of violence. The old fraternity among the military men and caudillos fell apart. Now Villa was the enemy of Obregón, and Zapata was the enemy of Venustiano Carranza. Now Celaya could mean not only a victory but a defeat for the revolutionaries.

Constitutionalism triumphed. Faithful to his realistic and moderate policy, Venustiano Carranza wanted to adapt the Constitution of 1857 to the new Mexican circumstances. It was a vain attempt. From his own ranks came Jacobins who believed that the revolution required a unity of new principles capable of producing a real nation. And this could only be made possible by adding a good dose of economic and social equality to the juridical equality of the old liberalism. Social rights would accompany the now undisputed individual rights; the basic theses of natural law would be revised in the light of a historical idea of man and his liberty, man and his property, and man in his relation to other men; finally, the state would abandon its role of mere supervisor of the social process and would become the chief promoter of its improvement. The constitutionalists of 1917 did not shrink before the unorthodoxy of their ideas, for they considered them to be nothing more than the simple expression of the great national needs. Carranza accepted the defeat suffered in the Congress of Querétaro and he was to be, when elected president, the first to serve under the new constitutional regime.

The social revolution got underway so slowly that what was considered the supreme achievement of the movement—no reelection—gave rise to new conflicts. How could the government accomplish in four short years the huge task of social transformation which was the obligation of the state? Carranza, convinced that his conduct of the government was correct, conceived the idea of perpetuating it through a stooge. But the same constitutional principle that was an obstacle to Carranza in continuing his work turned out to be the only sure brake, at least for a while, on the political ambitions of the new leaders and groups eager to impose their own ways of governing. As the moment approached for the change in government, Carranza gave all his support to a civilian candidate, claiming that it was necessary to block militarism from the presidency. The revolutionaries again fought among themselves and Carranza was destroyed.

Ten years after the start of the revolution, Madero, Zapata, and Carranza, the three leading figures of the first stage, no longer existed. The new generation of revolutionary caudillos advanced triumphantly to the forefront of national life. They tried almost feverishly to make up for lost time by inaugurating the stage of national reconstruction.

2

1921-1952

IN 1920 Mexico initiated what promised to be an era of peace. That year, after a brief interim civilian government that acted as a bridge between the latest armed uprising and the new institutional life, Álvaro Obregón occupied the presidency of the Republic. One of the most brilliant and without a doubt the most powerful of the military leaders who had emerged from the revolutionary movement, Obregón was elected after a makeshift campaign waged by barely embryonic political parties, which was more evidence of a series of good intentions than an expression of reality.

When Obregón was elected, most of his power was based on his having been a victorious caudillo. But the new president was shrewd enough to realize that his personal merits had neither won him the office nor would they sustain the entire weight of his administration. His personal success was to some extent that of his revolutionary faction—composed mainly of the middle class—which in turn could be explained by the capacity of such a group to represent, at least formally, all the sectors of the nation.

The success of the middle class was actually due to the fact that it possessed a broader social perspective and a greater ideological unity than the popular groups. The workers were few in number and divided in their doctrines, as had been demonstrated in the disconcerting and fleeting revolutionary episode of the "Red Battalions." But the confusion of social questions and their apparent quiescence during the first days of the Obregón regime were no

129

assurance that they would not come up at any moment as impera-
tives.

On the other hand, the victory of the ruling group, still
supported chiefly by arms, needed to be transformed into a true
social and political triumph, producing a genuinely national state
by being more representative and powerful than any of the conflicting interests. To achieve these ends, the constitutional compromise of 1917 had to be implemented by positive acts. Insofar as
the government responded to the needs and aspirations of the
peasants and the workers, the latter would identify with and support it. Also in this way, the sources of power would be other than
military.

National reconstruction really began in 1921. Agrarian reform
was put into operation, although slowly and intermittently. The
latifundium, now forbidden, began to yield to small property
which, according to official policy, was the best form of land
exploitation. This was accompanied by restitution and grants of
land for ejidos as a secondary solution. Thus, in spite of its
deficiencies, land redistribution became the basis of a more complex and productive economy, which would be the only guarantee
of success in the industrialization of Mexico.

Furthermore, although land distribution was not always carried out as broadly and rapidly as it should have been to meet the
needs of the peasants, it did arouse in them expectations that could
be channelled politically to establish a close alliance between the
nascent state and the rural population. The next step was to
organize the peasants into large associations, thereby giving
greater unity and effectiveness to their social force.

A similar procedure had to be followed with the workers, but
in their case taking into account a particular historical circumstance. From the beginning and in spite of its often anarchist
form, the labor movement had been so weak that it had turned to
the Mexican State for protection of its interests against frequently
foreign employers. In addition, labor leaders had been incorporated into the state apparatus at very high posts, so their
solidarity was fully guaranteed.

The state therefore acquired two powerful forces of socio-
political action; but the new popular organizations inevitably had

to suffer all the ideological fluctuations of the governments born of the revolution. Nevertheless, the effectiveness of these alliances was soon to be seen. In the struggle for power, armed uprisings had to depend almost exclusively on military support and were easily suppressed, to be exposed to the nation as acts of political adventurers who at best advocated a nominal democracy and an electoral contest that was unsuited to the new social democracy proclaimed by the government and demonstrated by its actions.

Such were the cases of Adolfo de la Huerta in 1923 and of Serrano and Gómez in 1927. Each attempt at rebellion, far from strengthening the army, always deprived it of some of its oldest and most powerful generals.

In 1924, with the new bases of political power established, Plutarco Elías Calles took office as president. During most of his government the already accepted directives of social action and political orthodoxy functioned—so much so that Mexico managed to emerge almost unscathed from the resurgence of one of the most deeply rooted problems in its history: the religious. Over the years, the new realities of society and of the economy necessarily produced some degree of skepticism and a desire for spiritual reform. Therefore, when the Church, failing to understand the changes that had taken place in the country, tried to stand in the way of freedom of conscience and broader educational possibilities, it remained almost isolated. Its cause was further weakened by the recent and extraordinary educational experiment of Vasconcelos, representing an integral humanism, which showed that the state could impart an education that did not conflict with any of man's vocations. Thus, the Cristero War was a painful and bloody episode, but nothing more.

Mexico was unquestionably transforming itself into a modern state. At the end of the Calles regime, there were signs of change in many spheres. When public works were constructed to develop the agricultural economy as well as health and education services, a flood of wealth began to create a national class which was both economically strong and with access to the structure of public power. Furthermore, the need for foreign credit for Mexico's growth had greatly moderated the nationalist attitudes maintained during the armed revolution.

Meanwhile, popular pressures for a more just society did not altogether cease and they were no less valid than the problems they expressed. The years known as the "Maximato" were especially ambiguous and fluctuated between adherence to and abandonment of the revolutionary tenets of 1917. Although the social revolution did not stop, it slowed down, particularly at the beginning of the 1930s.

At that time, Mexican political life underwent a drastic radical change. First Obregón and later Calles—two types of caudillo—were eliminated, paradoxically, by the very instruments of social control that had made them so powerful. After them, political power was institutionalized to the point where it hardly mattered who exercised it. Those who in 1928 assassinated Obregón had not understood that he was simply the visible head of the revolution made government; they thought they had halted or liquidated the revolution.

To the contrary, that same year an official party was created. The functions of this new political organization were many: to automatically confer power on the new men who, by the legal requirements of no-reelection, would take office; to avoid the anarchy of an electoral contest that, bloody or not, decimated or divided the revolutionary ranks; to permit the groups represented in the party itself to alternate or at least share in the power; and to limit or control the real contradictions in Mexican society, which frequently could be reduced to a mere ideological dispute.

The effectiveness of the party became evident, just a few months after it had been created, in the presidential campaign of 1929. The opposition candidate was Vasconcelos, who embodied the by-gone era of exceptional political figures. His superior intelligence and a personality that made him known internationally rendered him potentially dangerous. Moreover, his democratic demand had the merit of being a real debt of the revolution. His highly moral criticism pointed out the elements of corruption in the official Mexican world. But his social policy, notably weak, meant little to those who, without being a formal part of the government, had received far greater benefits than those promised by Vasconcelos and who now, within the government and in their new role as participants, hoped to increase these benefits. On the other hand, the official candidate, a minor political figure and an undistinguished personality transfigured by the magic of the party, appeared to be powerful and master of a social and economic program which truly reflected the national problems and offered adequate solutions. So with support skillfully induced from peasants and workers, Ortiz Rubio legalized his victory. But the ambiguity of the socio-political moment did not change and its first victim was the recently elected president, who soon had to resign.

In subsequent years the crisis worsened and although legislation was aimed at social improvement, and government measures actually were of popular benefit, everything was promoted unilaterally from the seat of power which, paradoxically, harshly repressed the freely expressed demands of rural and urban workers. The interim government of Abelardo Rodríguez, facing a situation of severe social tension, drafted a long-term program, the Six-Year Plan, so radical that it seemed unlikely to be implemented under the existing official policy.

With the Six-Year Plan as his platform, Lázaro Cárdenas undertook in December 1933 an electoral campaign of unprecedented geographical and social scope. The machinery of the official party operated with its customary efficiency and its candidate won an overwhelming majority of the popular vote. Lázaro Cárdenas became president of Mexico in 1934.

At the start of the new government, as in all the governments of Mexico, social positions were radicalized in an effort to force the president to define his doctrine as soon as possible. Social pressures rose. Breaking with the political style of the immediate past, Cárdenas sided with the popular movements. Confident of government support, first the workers and then the peasants bypassed their old organizations and leaders. By freeing popular social forces in this way, the government did not mean to relinquish its direction of them but simply to change their objectives.

However, these actions were not to be taken with impunity. The owners of vested interests, both Mexicans and non-Mexicans, long sheltered under the shadow of the "Jefe Máximo," persuaded the latter to condemn, in the name of the revolution, this dangerous and sterile agitation and to make veiled threats against the man considered responsible for the situation, the president of the Republic. The lines of battle within the power groups were drawn. The Cárdenas government would put to a test the broader and more resistant power base it had built by its concessions to the popular masses. The contest lasted almost three years and its crucial episodes were a violent cabinet crisis; the exiling of Calles, the strongman of Mexico; the neutralizing of the old labor and peasant associations by the creation of parallel ones; and the reorganization of the official party.

This last event confirmed the ability of the Cárdenas regime to assimilate and to evolve. To the workers and the peasants, the party added a large sector of the middle class, product of the revolution itself and chiefly embedded in the bureaucracy, as well as the army composed of a new generation with a new mentality, especially in its lower ranks. On the same bases of popular support, duly reinforced with a good measure of defensive nationalism, the government could deal with the powerful foreign investors. Through a series of agricultural expropriations, improvements for workers, and the recovery of railways and oil, it confirmed national sovereignty and established the real beginnings of economic independence.

Certainly, the regime of Lázaro Cárdenas occasionally adopted the language of socialism as its own. Nevertheless, in practice it followed the doctrine clearly formulated since 1906 by the Liberal Party and maintained more or less faithfully throughout the revolutionary process: the creation and development of a capitalist economy, but liberated from the social injustices it produces. However, the gravity of Mexico's problems precipitated many of its measures of social and economic policy, which in turn weakened their implementation. The counterattacks of those affected by the measures and even the danger of seeing its policy frustrated by an uncontrolled radicalization of the worker and peasant organizations forced the regime to adopt a more moderate tone, further emphasized at the legally inevitable moment of presidential change in 1940.

The political contest between Ávila Camacho and Almazán was particularly active and even violent to the point that civil war was feared. The rival forces clearly defined their positions. During the campaign the opposition drew on all its resources—the possibility of a foreign invasion to eliminate the threat of communism in Mexico, an attempted revolt, as well as the organization of real political parties. The official party made its considerable strength felt and Manuel Ávila Camacho became president.

The setting of the Second World War justified the new policy, proclaimed as one of national unity, although in fact it silenced social demands and favored the resurgence of the factors of power that had been weakened in the previous six-year period. The agrarian reform, once flourishing, now withered, as did labor movements. Foreign capital, tied more than ever for reasons of security and international strategy to national capital, became increasingly powerful and unrestrained. Still, the ideology of the Revolution was not entirely ignored by the Ávila Camacho regime, which adopted and carried out its objective of a capitalist economy, albeit at the expense of social justice.

After 1946, under the government of Miguel Alemán, the period initiated in the previous regime was consolidated. Historically and ideologically, the Alemán regime reappraised the Mexican revolutionary process and found it absurd. By distributing an uncertain, almost nonexistent wealth, previous regimes had created an illusion of progress. This misguided policy had to be discarded and a new direction inaugurated. Wealth had to be created before it could be distributed. Only in this way could Mexico leave its mistaken past behind and go beyond its revolution.

At that time the country experienced one of its great spurts of growth, which carried it to the verge of economic "take-off" and fulfillment of its long held and legitimate desire to be fully modern. So at first, the Alemán regime seemed to be right. The accumulation of capital furnished by the war and by a policy of indiscriminate acceptance of foreign investment generated a spectacular expansion of the Mexican economy. But to sustain and especially to increase the rate of growth of a dependent country required that someone within its boundaries pay for the progress. Those whom the Revolution had always claimed to be the benefi-ciaries of national wealth were supposed to dedicate themselves first to creating it. The agrarian reform was slowed down and the legal instruments guaranteeing it were modified. Worker movements were brutally suppressed and many of their leaders bought off in a

systematic policy of corruption. The official party was reorganized
to eliminate from its program any dangerous elements of social
reform.

The Alemán government, by weakening the bases of popular
support created by its predecessors, tilted precariously toward
other points of support. The Mexican State ran the risk of losing
its capacity to direct national life and of becoming a prisoner of
powerful economic interests.

VI. THE PRESENT

Daniel Cosío Villegas

TO 1972

HISTORIANS GENERALLY AGREE in dividing the study of the Mexican Revolution into three stages. The first was the "destructive," from 1910 to 1920, when the principal task was to do away with the old Porfirian regime and at least to conceive a theoretical framework for the Constitution of 1917, within which the new society created by the Revolution was supposed to emerge. The second, from 1921 to 1940, is called the "reformist" because this stage brought application of the agrarian reform; strengthening of the labor unions; revival of education and culture; and the founding of institutions like the Bank of Mexico, the National Bank of Agricultural Credit, and the Regional Schools of Agriculture, which would be the basis of the "new" Mexico. Finally, the third stage, from 1941 to 1970, has been called the stage of "consolidation" or "modernization," although a more graphic and descriptive name would be "Political Stability and Economic Progress."

Of course, any division of history into periods or stages is arbitrary. Therefore, it is not surprising that the stage of "political stability" really began in 1929, when the first official or government party was founded with the name Partido Nacional Revolucionario (National Revolutionary Party). Its initial objective was to settle power struggles not by arms, as had happened from 1910 to 1928, but by the civilized means of a purely political contest which would evolve as follows: all aspirants to any elective office could and should make their political campaign freely and openly within the Party; a duly convoked convention would measure the support received by each of the aspirants and would select the one who had

139

been most widely accepted; the convention would declare him to be the official Party candidate and he would be supported by his defeated rivals and by the entire Party.

Schism was the sign under which the Mexican Revolution was born and under which it lived until 1928. Barely had it begun in Chihuahua when Pascual Orozco and Francisco Villa refused to recognize the authority of Madero and even threatened to imprison him in order to eliminate him politically and physically. After Porfirio Díaz was defeated and the provisional government of Francisco León de la Barra established, the brothers Vázquez Gómez, who were the representatives of Madero in that government, quarreled publicly with the provisional president. A short time after Madero was elected constitutional president, his former lieutenant Pascual Orozco and these same brothers Vázquez Gómez, who had accompanied him from the very start of the anti-reelectionist movement, took up arms against him. With the birth of the constitutionalist movement led by Carranza, Villa expressed his lack of confidence in the revolutionary group of Sonora and a little later openly defied the authority of Carranza, whose official title was the very significant one of "First" Chief of the Constitutionalist Army. The Aguascalientes Convention, called after Huerta's defeat precisely to give unity to the governing action of Constitutionalism, followed suit. Madero and later Carranza both failed to join into a single group the revolutionaries of the north and south, especially the followers of Zapata.

During Carranza's four-year term as constitutional president, there was not a single day when the entire country was at peace, for there were always centers of armed rebellion against his authority. The disintegration of the revolutionary group became still more apparent during the presidential elections of 1920. Because no agreement had been reached on who was to succeed Carranza, General Álvaro Obregón decided to overthrow the president by a military coup. In the 1924 elections Adolfo de la Huerta led a revolt against President Obregón; and in the 1928 elections President Calles was challenged by Generals Francisco Serrano, Arnulfo R. Gómez, Francisco Manzo, and Gonzalo Escobar.

These military rebellions not only disrupted law and order in the country but they also destroyed what little material wealth

Mexico had managed to accumulate in its years of tranquility. Furthermore, they furnished the sad and depressing spectacle of the assassination of such great caudillos of the Revolution as Madero, Carranza, Obregón, and Serrano, as well as the execution of distinguished military commanders.

In contrast with this turbulent period, for the forty years from 1929 to 1970 presidential and local elections have been carried out peaceably. Although this healthy change cannot altogether be attributed to the founding of the "official" Party in 1929, the latter must be credited with resisting the incursions of time and especially divisions within the Party itself. General Juan Andreu Almazán in 1940, Ezequiel Padilla in 1946, and General Miguel Henríquez Guzmán in 1952 left the Party in order to oppose the officially designated candidates; but there was no breakdown of public order, the official candidates won their elections, and the Party rapidly repaired the gaps produced by these electoral adventures. It should be added that in subsequent presidential elections there has been absolutely no discord.

The military revolts of Madero against Porfirio Díaz and of Venustiano Carranza and his constitutionalists against Victoriano Huerta, as well as the armed struggles among the various revolutionary factions (Obregón supporters against Carranza; de la Huerta supporters against Obregón; and Serrano, Manzo, Gómez, and others against Calles) inevitably had grave economic consequences. On the one hand, railways and telephone communications were destroyed and on the other hand, Mexico failed to keep up with the economic progress being made by countries at peace. Given these two circumstances it is not to be wondered that over the next twenty or thirty years the national economy either declined or barely advanced from the level it had reached in 1910. After the first outbreak of the revolution, economic recovery began late and proceeded slowly.

It is significant that historians divide Mexico's economic development into a period of "uneven economic growth" from 1910 to 1935 and a period of "sustained economic growth" from 1935 to 1970. A further distinction is made between the first five years, when the national economy plummeted, and the years of its gradual recovery until 1935. For example, the value of mining output, then the most important sector of Mexican exports, took thirteen years to return to its 1910 level. Agricultural and livestock output fell to half of what they had been in the last year of the Porfiriato. The single exception was petroleum, which rose in production from around 30 million pesos to 1 800 million.

The country's economy had barely begun to recover when a new calamity struck. This was the Great Depression of 1929-1933 which, originating in the United States, rapidly spread to all the world, including Mexico. The sale of Mexican products abroad was reduced in 1932 to only a third of what it had been two years earlier, and purchases abroad were similarly reduced. Government revenues dropped by a fourth and expenditures therefore had to be cut back drastically.

About 1936 this situation began to change. Agriculture, for example, which had remained almost stationary from the end of the Porfiriato until 1935, began to develop at a rate higher than the rest of the national economy. This remarkable advance was partly achieved by extending the land under cultivation from 15 million to 24 million hectares (40 to 65 million acres) between 1930 and 1960. It was also due to the use of better agricultural techniques, especially of fertilizer and improved, high-yielding varieties of seeds, as well as to large-scale irrigation works. The development of industry after 1936 was also striking, with the value of manufactured goods rising almost 8 percent annually and with a similar expansion in construction and electric power.

The result of these and other factors was that after 1940, the Mexican economy developed by more than 6 percent annually, which was higher than the average growth rate in Latin America, even including such favorably endowed countries as Argentina, Brazil, and Venezuela.

But not all was paradise or eternal. A study made in the early sixties, the first of its kind, revealed that the benefits of this great economic progress were very unevenly distributed. Whereas 10 percent of the population received almost half the national income, 40 percent had barely 14 percent. A little later it was discovered that the imbalance in economic development was not only vertical according to the different layers of the social pyramid, but it was also regional. States like Jalisco, Nuevo León, and Puebla had prospered, others had stagnated, and the vast majority has seen their economic situation deteriorate. A further misfortune was that a greater number of people lived in stagnant or backward states than in the prosperous ones; and even within the poorest states there were zones that were worse off than the state average. Nothing illustrated this regional imbalance better than the Federal District. With a territory smaller than any other state, it contained more than twice the number of inhabitants in the most populous state and its budget was eighteen times that of Nuevo León, the richest state. It was found, moreover, that in Mexico industrial workers received substantially higher wages than agricultural labor and that within the latter, farmers on irrigated lands earned more than farmers in the less productive Bajío region.

It has, then, become urgent to redress the inequities of Mexico's economic development and to make this possible in the face of a series of demographic problems that have arisen since 1940. From 1930 to 1940 Mexico's population increased by 2.7 percent annually: the birth rate was 5 percent, while the death rate exceeded 2 percent. However, in the 1960s, as a result of a considerable decline in mortality, the death rate was less than 1 percent, while the birth rate remained at over 4 percent, so that population growth reached 3.4 percent per year. This means that although Mexico had more men and women to work and create wealth, it also had many more mouths to feed. Another demographic problem is what is called the "composition" of population or its grouping by age. Almost half the population (49.9 percent) was outside the labor market because it was less than 15 or more than 65 years old. This means that in 1970, 25 million Mexicans had to work to support and educate not only themselves but also the 25 million who could not do so because of age. Finally, the other great problem is the urban concentration of the population, its steady rural-urban migration, and the inability of the city to give them all employment, education, medical care, and other services.

Another object of study and observation is political stability, which was the other distinctive feature of the most recent stage of the Mexican Revolution. Peace and order have continued relatively undisturbed, and both local and national elections have proceeded normally. But Mexico has undergone radical changes since the

mid-30s that require it to adapt its political life to the new circumstances. Progress in communication and transportation has
brought Mexicans much closer together so that there now exists
among them a community of ideas and feelings that formerly were
fragmented. The multiplication of schools and the increasing number of people attending them have awakened in today's Mexican a
more aware and demanding civic conscience. All this engenders
the desire to participate in the public life of the country and to
democratize it at every level. The official Party shoud therefore
open itself to the renovating current of youth and it should also
encourage political parties of the opposition in order to give the
Mexican voter a real choice between different programs and
various candidates.

If a moral can be drawn from what has been said here, it is that
Mexico has entered a new stage in its life and that each and every
one of its citizens should do his best in his respective field of action
to help solve the many and difficult problems confronting his
country.

Bibliography

BRANDENBURG, Frank. *The Making of Modern Mexico*. Englewood Cliffs, N. J., Prentice-Hall, 1964.

CORNELIUS, Wayne. *Politics and the Migrant Poor in Mexico City*. California, Stanford University Press, 1975.

ECKSTEIN, Susan. *The Poverty of Revolution, the State, and the Urban Poor in Mexico*. Princeton, N. J., University of Princeton Press, 1977.

HANKE, Lewis. *Aristotle and the American Indians. A Study in Race Prejudice in the Modern World*. Bloomington, Indiana University Press, 1975.

HANSEN, Roger. *The Politics of Mexican Development*. Baltimore, Johns Hopkins University Press, 1971.

LEWIS, Oscar. *The Children of Sánchez: An Autobiography of a Mexican Family*. New York, Vintage Books, 1961.

PADGETT, Leon Vincent. *The Mexican Political System*. Boston, Houghton Mifflin, 1966.

POWELL, Tom G. *Mexico and the Spanish Civil War*. Albuquerque, University of New Mexico Press, 1981.

RUIZ, Ramón Eduardo. *Mexico, the Challenge of Poverty and Illiteracy*. San Marino, California, The Huntington Library, 1963.

SCOTT, Robert. *Mexican Government in Transition*. Chicago, University of Illinois Press, 1959.

SMITH, Peter S. *Labyrinths of Power: Political Recruitment in Twentieth-Century Mexico*. Princeton, New Jersey, Princeton University Press, 1979.

VERNON, Raymond. *The Dilemma of Mexico's Economic Development: The Roles of the Private and the Public Sector*. Cambridge, Mass., Harvard University Press, 1963.

—— and Albert L. MICHAELS. *Revolution in Mexico: Years of Upheaval, 1910-1940*. New York, A. Knopf, 1969.

——, WILKIE, and James Wallace. *The Mexican Revolution: Federal Expenditure and Social Change Since 1910*. Los Angeles, University of California Press, 1970.

VII. YEARS OF CRISIS, YEARS OF OPPORTUNITY

Lorenzo Meyer

1970-1980

IN A WAY, the history of the 1970's began in 1968, for this was the year the political and social system handed down from the 1910 Revolution was severely tested. From July to October, Mexico City was the scene of massive demonstrations by students and professors stemming from incidents of violence in the secondary schools that had been exacerbated by repressive police action. Not since 1957-58, when force was used against striking teachers and railway workers—especially against the latter—had the legitimacy of the political course taken by the government been questioned.

By demanding that the democratic spirit of the 1917 Constitution be respected, the 1968 movement, without being openly revolutionary, condemned the government's authoritarian bias and its corporative political organization. The protests also called for a re-examination of the economic growth model adopted after the Second World War. This model not only had further skewed income distribution and failed to create the jobs intended to keep up with the growing population, but, in spite of rapid industrialization and agricultural modernization, had made Mexico increasingly dependent on external factors, including new ones such as technology. Although not presented as such, the 1968 movement was clearly a protest against the major features of the mixed economy, or at least as this had developed in recent years. The students, who were mainly middle class, could not gain the support of the workers, still less of the *campesinos*; throughout the crisis, these two sectors remained pillars of the political system, rejecting all efforts of the young people to win them over.

149

The brutal repression of the protesters, which culminated in the October 2nd massacre in the Square of the Three Cultures in Tlatelolco, put an end to the "holding of the streets" by the students. Although most of the academic community withdrew to its natural stronghold, the universities, its critical mood was transmitted to succeeding student generations or was expressed in more or less penetrating analyses of the system's "dark areas." Criticism of headlong development and authoritarian government literally exploded between 1971 and 1980, dampening the triumphant spirit of Mexico's political and economic leaders.

The consequences of 1968 were not limited to the so-called "crisis of conscience" and "consciousness of crisis." There were also those who believed that the repression left no option but to confront violence with violence, and this took several forms. The guerrilla in Mexico was a phenomenon of the 70s, especially of the first half. The more ideological urban guerrilla operated in Mexico's large cities, while rural guerrillas were found mainly in Guerrero, a state plagued with local problems and where violence was already endemic. Although they tried to make contact, the two groups were actually following different paths, and their eventual dispersal by government security forces closed off this possibility to the opposition. In 1977 the López Portillo administration tried to lessen the political cost of the operation by granting a broad amnesty to political prisoners.

The present Mexican political system has shown itself to be flexible in its treatment of protesters; it has generally preferred co-optation to repression. In 1971 the government opened the way to negotiation. President Echeverría joined the critics in attacking the philosophy and practice of the "developmentalist policy"—especially the so-called "stabilizing development"—because of the social injustices that it had accepted and fomented. From the pinnacle of power came condemnations of those who "betrayed the Revolution's ideals," of imperialism, and even of capitalism. Although this rhetoric—which had populist and neo-Cardenist undertones—was not translated into fundamental changes, it certainly caused considerable concern among some conservative sectors.

Part of Echeverría's response to the events of 1968 was to extend more financial grants to the universities; to accept and even encourage the formation of small leftist organizations like the Mexican Workers Party and the Socialist Workers Party; and to free most of the participants in the 1968 disturbances, some of whom were even given government jobs. For a time the media was also allowed greater scope to criticize; but at the end of his administration in 1976, Echeverría, who had made freedom of expression central to his "opening to democracy," abruptly lost patience with his critics and decided that their sharp and unremitting attacks should be curtailed. In particular, he was instrumental in the dismissal of the editors of *Excélsior*, Mexico's most important national newspaper. Nonetheless, the limited ground gained by the critics was not to be lost.

Under José López Portillo, who took office in December 1976 in the midst of a new crisis of confidence that was due mainly to economic and financial difficulties, rhetoric was toned down. While acknowledging the failure of developmentalist economics, his administration continued to search for a legitimate solution to the problem presented by the existence of a weak but organized and active opposition. In 1979, by means of legislative reform dealing with political parties and the electoral process, the government permitted two left-wing parties (the Mexican Communist and the Socialist Workers) and one right-wing party (the Mexican Democratic) to be registered and to receive all the concomitant benefits. This step was accompanied by changes in the law that increased the number of minority representatives in the Chamber of Deputies on a proportional basis. In this way, Congress was opened to the opposition, although the official Institutional Revolutionary Party, or PRI, was assured of keeping its majority in the Chamber of Deputies and its monopoly in the Senate. Furthermore, its control over all the state governorships and congresses and over the great majority of city halls remained unshaken. The so-called political reform consisted essentially in making room for a limited but institutional participation by the opposition, precisely so that the latter would not feel excluded and resort to illegal and violent activities.

Although the political crisis of the 70s dated from 1968 and the economic crisis began in 1973-74, they converged in the second half of the 70s. There had already been warnings that the import-substitution-based industrialization started during the Second World War would reach a dead end. The crux of the problem was that the possibilities of replacing imports of durable and nondurable consumer goods by domestic output would eventually be exhausted and that preparations should be made to enter a more complex stage aimed at producing intermediate goods on a large scale and developing the still incipient production of capital goods. It had also been seen that Mexico should promote outward growth through the export of manufactured goods, in order to overcome its almost total dependence on agricultural and mineral exports; but Mexico's industrial plant was inadequate and inefficient, and only in a few items could it compete on the international market.

Worldwide inflation began to be felt in Mexico in 1973, and by the following year it was firmly established. The remarkable price stability that had been maintained since the 1950s went by the board. Exports and net income from tourism did not increase as rapidly as imports, which raised the balance-of-payments deficits to alarming heights; it went from 891 million dollars on current account in 1971 to 3.7 billion dollars in 1975. In financial circles, loss of confidence lowered private investment and initiated an outflow of foreign exchange. The government borrowed huge sums of money abroad, chiefly from private banking institutions in the United States and Western Europe, which pushed its external debt up from 4.2 billion dollars in 1971 to 11.6 billion in 1975.

This strategy obviously could not be continued for very long; moreover, the inflation fueled by the swelling financial deficit of the public sector meant that the peso was seriously overvalued. Land expropriations in 1976, which were considered by many to be improper, accelerated the dollarization of the banking and financial economy and spurred the open flight of capital, even from small savings accounts. Floating the peso was thus made inevitable and the decision was taken on August 31, 1976, the eve of President Echeverría's last annual report to Congress. The fixed exchange rate of 12.50 pesos to the dollar fell immediately to about 20 pesos and later to 22 pesos, or a 37.5 to 43.25 percent drop in dollar terms.

In these circumstances, there was doubt both at home and abroad about the viability of what only ten years earlier had been called the Mexican Miracle. Distrust of the political and economic system became dangerously widespread. Hope for an immediate, if not basic, solution arose when it was announced that new deposits of oil and gas had been discovered; the figures for proven reserves went up from 5.4 billion barrels in 1973, to 11 billion in 1977, reaching 60 billion in 1980. The authorities decided that PEMEX (Petróleos Mexicanos) should take advantage of the dramatic increase in world prices; official policy was to produce enough oil to satisfy expanding domestic energy requirements and also to export as much as was needed to reduce the huge balance-of-payments deficit—worsened by the recent and unprecedented rise in food imports—but without allowing the economy to be distorted by the flood of new financial resources, which would be difficult to convert quickly into real output.

The figure finally adopted as production "platform" or ceiling, after several revisions, was 2.7 million barrels per day, of which about half was intended for domestic consumption and the rest for export. Rather than turn Mexico into an "oil-producing country," oil, which had been nationalized since 1938, was to be used as a means of correcting major structural defects in the Mexican economy—that is, to speed up the creation of jobs, to broaden the industrial base and achieve industrial efficiency, to attain self-sufficiency in food, to expand the transportation network, and to improve the educational and social welfare systems. The oil boom would itself generate larger tax revenues and would promote private investment in industry, so that by the next century, when Mexico would have depleted its hydrocarbon resources, it would already have consolidated a solid and permanent foundation for industrial and agricultural wealth. This was the objective of the National Development Plan issued by the government in 1980. The success of such an important project was by no means assured as Mexico advanced into the 1980s.

The long-standing income-concentration trends were intensified in 1971-1980 due to soaring inflation, inadequate tax reforms, and failure to tackle the basic structural problems of the economy, especially the low productivity of large sectors of agriculture. According to a survey conducted in 1977 by the Ministry of Programming and Budget, low-income families representing 50 percent of the population received only 13.5 percent of total available income, while the top 10 percent enjoyed 46 percent.

It should not be surprising that the greater latitude afforded the opposition parties by the political reforms, as well as inflation and other related factors, served to strengthen independent organized labor—in particular, the Independent Workers Unity, the Electricians Democratic Line, the Single Union of Nuclear Industry Workers, the Authentic Workers Front, the university unions, and some of the unions organized in large private businesses. This opposition, although significant, was in no way a threat to government control of most of the labor movement organized through the Workers Congress, which continued to be centered in the CTM (Workers Confederation of Mexico). In actual fact, and in spite of several conflicts with President Echeverría at the start of his six-year term, the CTM remained a bulwark of the official PRI party, the government, and the system, precisely because it was able, in the face of inflation and recession, to persuade its members to accept the wage ceilings established in consultation with the International Monetary Fund in 1976, which were essential if the economic situation was to be managed in the short run and if the rate of inflation was to be moderated.

Control of organized labor was only one side of the problem. According to recent estimates, there are about 5 million unionized workers. When to these are added another 5 million belonging to the CNC (National Peasant Confederation), the CNOP (National Confederation of Popular Organizations), and other organizations that are also corporative members of PRI, it turns out that 50 percent of the labor force is organized. The remainder are for the most part made up of the underemployed and unemployed—that is, the marginal population. If these sectors had been able to join together to press their demands for jobs, housing, health care, and other services, the system would probably not have been able to cope with them. It was to some degree the task of PRI organizations and the government to continue filling this void by means of relatively inexpensive rural employment programs, health care, the creation of some urban infrastructure, programs to legalize the situation of squatter settlements, the formation of urban settler associations, and the co-optation of natural leaders. The opposition parties, especially those on the left, have not been able to make much progress in organizing this vast apolitical mass, even though, in principle, the marginal population owed little, if any, loyalty to the government and it should have been easily enlisted into the ranks of those rejecting the *status quo*.

In the 1970s unemployment became the prime concern in a country having a population that increased from 50.6 million in 1970 to 70 million in 1980—notwithstanding official family planning programs and various social and cultural factors that were beginning to motivate couples to have fewer children. Since 1970, the birth rate has been declining and by 1980 the rate of population growth had been reduced from 3.6 percent per year to less than 2.8 percent.

Until recently, Mexico was a rural country where the backwardness of the production systems meant that unemployment was disguised by subsistence economies. By 1970, however, 45 percent of the population lived in agglomerations of more than 15 000 people, and by 1980 this had risen to more than 50 percent. The seemingly uncontrollable flood of migration from countryside to cities intensified the many already existing urban problems, particularly in the metropolitan area of Mexico City—which by the end of the 70s had 14 million inhabitants—as well as in Monterrey, Guadalajara, and Tijuana, and even in smaller cities like Coatzacoalcos and Acapulco.

Most Mexicans no longer worked directly on the land. In 1977 only 40 percent of the labor force was engaged in agricultural activities. One consequence was that most of the young people entering the labor force had to find work in industry or in services; but employment in the latter expanded slowly and the demand was increasingly for skilled or semi-skilled workers rather than workers without skills or education such as those coming from rural areas. The greater participation of women in the economically active population also reduced job opportunities for men. Furthermore, in few countries has the working-age population expanded so swiftly in a sluggish and structurally unbalanced economic system.

The relative neglect of the countryside in recent years did more than swell the rural exodus attracted by the higher wages offered in Mexican cities and in the United States. Without the incentive of price supports or improvement of agricultural conditions in the less favored but more populated areas, the production of food and some raw materials fell far behind demand. No longer able to supply its own food requirements, Mexico had to resort to the massive importation of grain, powdered milk, sugar, and other basic consumer goods. Discussion of the kind of land ownership best suited to increase production revived the debate between supporters and opponents of the ejido. The government decided not to alter the mixed structure of rural property, more out of political than economic motives. In any event, by the end of the decade the government was clearly making every effort to revitalize agriculture by raising price supports for certain food products, improving the rural credit system, introducing farm machinery, and converting grazing into crop land; in other words, it was trying to make agriculture a rational option for labor and capital. At the beginning of 1980 all these policies were incorporated into an ambitious project, SAM (Mexican Food System), which numbered among its medium-term goals to make the country once again relatively self-sufficient in food, to improve the storage and market-ing of farm produce, and to raise the nutrition levels of large sectors of the urban and rural populations.

The 1970s witnessed significant changes in Mexico's foreign policy, which had been defensive and, to some extent, passive. Under post-revolutionary governments, Mexico stayed in the back-ground at international forums. When President Echeverría took office in December 1970, he let it be known that his administration would continue this practice. Nonetheless, a short time later his government began to play an active and different role on the international scene. The main reason may have been the belief that the United States had lost interest in Mexico and that, regardless of geopolitical factors, Mexico had better look for new links abroad. In any event, the "special relationship" between the United States and Mexico that had been engendered by the Second World War was gradually disappearing, as demonstrated by some of the actions taken by the United States: in 1960, abruptly and without warning, Washington ordered a border check on day-to-day tourist crossings in order to force Mexico to step up its campaign against drug traffic; in 1971 no attention was paid to a Mexican request that its products be exempted from the 10 percent import tax levied by the United States.

Confronted by a U.S. attitude that he interpreted as negative and irreversible, President Echeverría decided that Mexico should associate with the Third World nations in a concerted effort to wrest from the developed countries the economic concessions required by the dependent and periphery economies. Mexicans were to be made aware that their country was also subject to the conditions prevailing in the underdeveloped world and that it would have to overcome the same international obstacles. After this decision was taken, nationalist and anti-imperialist traditions were no longer considered imprudent and Mexico pursued a position of leadership that in December 1974 culminated in the adoption by the United Nations General Assembly of the Charter of Economic Rights and Duties of States—a Mexican proposal that contained the economic principles upheld by most of the underdeveloped countries in the name of international justice.

At the inter-American level, Mexico regarded the OAS (Organization of American States) as practically useless and lent its enthusiastic support to SELA (Latin American Economic System), which was organized to coordinate and maintain prices of the leading raw materials exported by the region, to promote joint activities, and to establish Latin American transnational corporations (including Cuba) such as a Caribbean merchant marine to compete with the huge international companies and reduce the cost of ocean transport. Mexico also reactivated its relations with socialist Cuba and openly backed Salvador Allende's Popular Unity government in Chile. When Allende was overthrown, Mexico broke relations with the military junta and opened its doors to political refugees not only from Chile but from other Latin American countries. In 1979, Mexico broke relations with the Somoza regime and subsequently recognized the Nicaraguan revolutionary government.

At the domestic level, Mexico tried to modify the rules of the game for direct private foreign investment and to loosen its bonds of dependence. This policy resulted in laws on registry of the transfer of technology, the use and exploitation of patents and brand names (1972), and the promotion of Mexican investment and regulation of foreign investment (1973).

But the economic and financial bases of Echeverría's effort to increase Mexico's independence were not sound, and the 1976 crisis brought these international activities to a sudden halt. The López Portillo government had to seek the backing of the International Monetary Fund and indirectly of the United States to create a climate of confidence in the country's economic viability. Not long after withdrawing from the world scene, Mexico recovered the momentum of its economic growth thanks to the rapid development of its oil resources; and the international capital markets stopped worrying about its possible insolvency.

Tensions again rose with the United States over the sale of natural gas and the presence in that country of several million undocumented Mexican workers; this time, however, Mexico entered negotiations newly armed with oil. Although Mexico was vulnerable because of its massive food imports from the United States and the threat of a hardening of U.S. policy on undocumented workers, it did not hesitate to use its oil to gain ground in Central America, which had traditionally been a U.S. zone of influence. Neither did it hesitate to strengthen its political and even economic relations with Cuba and to actively try to diversify its oil markets in order to create ties with other industrial powers and obtain technology for new industries. Mexico thus sought to give greater flexibility to its international policy.

At the end of the 1970s, Mexico seemed to have reasserted itself as a medium power and to have reduced its dependence on its powerful neighbor to the north. In the long run, the success of this enterprise would be the result of not only decisions made, but also the ability of the group in power to solve Mexico's grave problems by achieving an efficient economy, revitalizing agriculture, expanding employment, opening the way to increased democracy in political life, and making income distribution more equitable—in short, by a reaffirmation of the legitimacy of the system.

GENERAL BIBLIOGRAPHY

BAZANT, Jean. *A Concise History of Mexico: From Hidalgo to Cárdenas (1850-1940)*. New York, Cambridge University Press, 1977.

FERNÁNDEZ, Justino. *A Guide to Mexican Art: From its Beginnings to the Present*. Translated by Joshua C. Taylor. Chicago, University of Chicago Press, 1978.

MAYO, Samuel H. *A History of Mexico: From Pre-Columbian to Present*. Englewood Cliffs, N. J., Prentice-Hall, 1978.

MEYER, Michael C. and William L. SHERMAN. *The Course of Mexican History*. New York, Oxford University Press, 1979.

SIMPSON, Lesley Byrd. *Many Mexicos*. Berkeley, University of California Press, 1961.

A Compact History of Mexico
se terminó de imprimir en mayo de 2004
en los talleres de Reproducciones y Materiales,
S.A. de C.V., Presidentes 189-A, col. Portales
03300 México, D.F. Se imprimieron 2 000 ejemplares
más sobrantes para reposición.
Cover: Mónica Diez-Martínez.